Scaling The Heights

Nicholas Correa

Title: Scaling The Heights

Author's Name: Nicholas Correa

nvcorrea@gmail.com
www.nvcorrea.com

ISBN: 978-93-5906-100-9

Price: ₹ 250/-

First Edition Published in 2023

Navi Mumbai, Maharashtra, India

DEDICATION

I dedicate this book to the Society of the Divine Word popularly known as SVD for its role and impact on my life.

CONTENTS

PREFACE AND ACKNOWLEDGEMENT

'Scaling The Heights' is a non-fiction and Self-Help Book that illustrates the engineering of life influenced by various pillars and columns. The book throws adequate light on self-discovery, personal growth, and professional development. Discovering one's calling and interest, followed by commitment is the primary step in scaling any heights.

Consumerism, sophisticated lifestyle, and corporate culture have impacted society and the way of thinking. Therefore, it is crucial to understand the existing realities to adapt to changes in life while scaling the heights. The vivid examples and stories make the book thought-provoking and fascinating for readers, professionals, students, teachers, and people from all walks of life and help them to scale the heights of life in the existing realities.

Life is like scaling heights or climbing a ladder. It need not be essentially continuous climbing. There can be unforeseen withdrawals and quite often the impact of the sophisticated standard of living comes on the way as an obstruction. One needs to learn how to tackle them.

One can use any suitable tool to scale the heights. Ladders are everywhere, and there are different forms of ladders to fit different needs. Some want to scale heights on their own, many want to do it at the expense of others and, some want to scale the heights to take others along, however, a few, scale the heights to serve. What is your purpose in scaling the heights?

I express, my gratitude to God Almighty for inspiring me to write this book. I thank my family for their constant support. I also take this opportunity to express my gratitude to one and all who have helped me in small or little ways to write this book.

ABOUT THE AUTHOR

Nicholas Correa, the author of the Book 'Scaling The Heights' is primarily an educationalist. He is an excellent academician, efficient administrator, motivational speaker, author, and trainer.

He is the founder Principal of New Horizon Public School, Navi Mumbai, and has been associated with New Horizon Group of Schools since her inception as Principal and Director.

He is innovative in his approach to education and has created a meaningful difference in the lives of thousands of students and so many teachers and parents. He is an ardent facilitator, an effective team builder, fond of children, and known for his innovative and creative ideas in the education sector.

Many of his articles have been published in Times of India-NIE, Hindustan Times-HT Next, The Hindu, and various other magazines and blogs. He has authored a book titled, "Crossing the Fence". He believes in making a meaningful difference in the lives of people through his writings.

1

INTRODUCTION

"Create a ladder of values and priorities in your life, reminding yourself of what really matters to you."

Scaling the Heights is a life's journey to reach the destination. Everyone has a different journey from others. A ladder represents a series of steps or stages that leads to a higher level. As you climb the ladder you grow and progress in life. You can recognize the progress you have made when you work towards the goals. The progress you make while scaling the heights motivates you to keep going. What does scaling the heights, mean to you?

"Some people are at the top of the ladder, some are in the middle, still more are at the bottom, and a whole lot more don't even know there is a ladder." All are called to scale heights and be successful in life. No one sets out to fail however, in the process we see many people failing, losing hope, and struggling. One cannot scale the heights without taking risks. It always comes with a price.

The height indicates growth and progress. Some scale the heights effectively only for accumulating material wealth which can be called growth. Many others grow in material wealth and also imbibe values in the process which can be called progress. However, only a few progressive people are successful because they scale heights beyond the realms of growth and progress.

There is a misconception about understanding the meaning of success. Success doesn't restrict to becoming millionaires or billionaires or achieving a certain position. It can be a requirement in the process of achieving success in many of the goals. However, success is not just about imbibing growth and progress with values but understanding the meaning of life and working towards its mysteries.

Many people scale the heights of success in their respective fields even without being multi-millionaires or with limited resources and money. Some are successful students, some are successful farmers, some are successful shoemakers, some are successful milkmen, some are successful hygiene workers, some are successful homemakers, some are successful monks, etc. Success is not an event; it is a journey. The parameters of success in life are purely subjective.

Generally, humans are ambitious and want to go ahead. All those who are successful in life are ambitious and committed. It is essential to dream about what you want to become and set realistic goals, adapt to situations, and make appropriate plans. When you are serious about your dreams and aspirations and goals, they drive you to scale the heights of your growth and progress.

Great scalers always set their goals and execute their plans to achieve their dreams and goals. They are serious about what they want to achieve. Scaling the heights of life is not an event, but a continuous process. As you scale the heights you may come across both positive and negative situations and people. In the same manner, you too may embrace both positives and negatives in the process.

Leaders are efficient in scaling heights. However, their progress depends on whether their ladder or the tool they select is leaned on the right wall and their success depends on whether they are taking their team along. The rung of the ladder is meant to hold one's feet and enable others to put higher.

Leadership plays an important role in an organization. The success of the team depends on the mindset of the leaders and their openness to creativity and innovation. While scaling the heights, a good leader takes along even the team members. A good leader can create a positive attitude and bring in changes easily for the success of the organization. You cannot force anyone up a ladder without one being willing to climb.

2

DISCOVER YOUR CALLING

"Everybody has a calling. And your real job in life is to figure out as soon as possible what that is, who you were meant to be, and to begin to honour that in the best way possible for yourself."

"Love your calling with passion. It is the meaning of your life."
                                        -Auguste Rodin

Gaur Gopal Das was born on 24 December 1973 into a middle-class family in Pune. He graduated from the College of Engineering, Pune in 1995 in Electrical Engineering. He started his career as an electrical engineer at Hewlett-Packard. While working here he felt he was not able to make a difference in the lives of people through his profession.

He was not satisfied with his job because he felt that something was missing. A year later in 1996, Gaur Gopal Das resigned from his job and joined the International Society for Krishna Consciousness (ISKCON) and became a monk and lifestyle engineer (life coach).

Gaur Gopal Das always wanted to make a difference in the lives of people, and he discovered it as his calling. He felt that he could do it effectively through spirituality; he was also highly inclined to the spiritual path. He felt making a profound difference was hard whereas making money was easy. So, he chose the spiritual path to spread positivity among the masses and make a meaningful difference in their lives.

You will not know what to pursue when you lack clarity about yourself and struggle to make choices or take important decisions about your life. Awareness of personal values outlines your sense of 'self'. Your values describe your qualities and your priorities.

Your values support your actions and are the driving force behind what really matters to you. They represent your identity. For example, the way you treat others. You will get carried away by circumstances and other people when you lack self-awareness. Consequently, this will drive you away from your potential and calling/vocation.

Your traits, abilities, likes, dislikes, beliefs, conduct, and the factors that motivate you, contribute to your self-image and your unique identity. You may not consciously spend time thinking about your identity. Your 'self' represents your features and your characteristics. Self-knowledge makes it easier to accept your 'self'. Knowing 'who you are?' helps you to live with a purpose and develop your contacts and relationships.

What is calling?

Do you wake up in the morning with the thought that you are going to do something you enjoy? Do you go to bed feeling contented with your day's work? Several studies show that only a very small section of people enjoyed what they did each day. It is essential to engage in a job, hobby, or passion which gives you satisfaction. Hence it is crucial to discover your calling when you pursue your job, hobby, or passion.

Your calling can be sharing your talents and innate gifts for the good of society or using your abilities in service. 'Calling' is discovering and pursuing your actual and innate passion, skill, or vocation. It is a vocation or profession in which one usually engages. According to Frederick Buechner, "Vocation is where our greatest passion meets the world's greatest need."

The Importance of Calling:

According to Tomas Merton, "Vocation does not come from a voice out there calling me to be something I am not. It comes from a voice in here calling me to be the person I was born to be." Is it important to have a calling? Does your job align with your calling? Generally, most people choose their careers following the bandwagon without analyzing whether their job is going to keep them happy and create meaning in their life.

Most people choose a career keeping in mind the kind of compensation they are going to receive. There are so many others who are confused to choose their career. At the same time, there is a small section of people who find a career that gives them meaning and happiness.

People who choose their careers based on their calling are more satisfied with their life, health, and job. For example, Sunil Gavaskar, Sachin Tendulkar, Virat Kolhi, and many others chose cricket not only because it gave them a plum career, but because it was their passion and calling. They loved cricket and lived cricket.

Generally, for many people work is a job, a source of income, and a stimulation for reward. For some, work is their job or career ingrained in the concept of service. For some people work is the source of income for living and leads to a higher purpose in life. What does your work mean to you?

Your calling always need not be your job. It can be a hobby, service, volunteering, raising a family, and so on. It doesn't mean that you need to change your career or job to comply with your calling. You can integrate your innate gifts and passions into the job you are already doing. According to Nicholas Weiler, "Fulfilling careers seldom happen by chance.

People who find personally meaningful vocations do so because they assume responsibility for their journeys."

Many people assume calling is a one-time event. A call is a way of expressing your understanding of the plan for your life. Your calling involves your heart and mind. It engages your natural gifts and the issues you are concerned about most. Your passion guides your goals and directs your energy. Your innate gifts and passions help you to find your purpose in life.

According to Dr. Jonas Salk, "To become devoted to a calling, to have a sense of responsibility, and have hopes and aspirations are all part of being human. To have no calling, no sense of responsibility, no hopes or aspirations, is to be outside of life."

How do you find your life's calling?

Oprah Winfrey the famous American Talk show host once said, "I believe there's a calling for all of us. I know that every human being has value and purpose. The real work of our lives is to become aware. And awakened. To answer the call."

Did you ever ask your inner self what you want to become in life or just moved with the flow? What is your life's path? What do you want to pursue in life? What is your calling or vocation in life? You will receive mixed responses if you ask people whether they have found their calling in life.

Many people struggle to find their calling or vocation. It's not always easy to find out what you want to do with your life. When you look within and begin to recognize your passions and values you come closer to identifying your calling.

Mahatma Gandhi gave up his covetable career as a barrister in South Africa and identified his calling to lead the freedom movement in India. Mother Teresa as a nun was a teacher, and Principal of a school. She gave up the teaching profession and completely dedicated her life to the destitute and, dying and contented serving them. Sindhutai Sapkal herself being destitute became a renowned social worker. Ratan TATA despite being a great Industrialist found his calling to be a philanthropist.

Some of the techniques to discover your calling:

1. Identifying activities that give you satisfaction	5. Channel your calling into a career
2. Try to experiment with different options	6. Pursue your calling as a hobby
3. Ask others what they could see you doing	7. Notice dreams and signs
4. Follow your heart and intuition	8. Give time for creative expression
	9. Be patient

1. **Identifying activities that give you satisfaction**: Introspect on your childhood days' aspirations. Ask yourself how you would like to spend your time every day. If you are already doing a job, find ways to spend your time after your office hours or on weekends that give you meaning.

   It can be volunteering in some social work, coaching less privileged children, creating awareness among the public on water conservation, etc. Anything that makes you miserable is not worth your time. Hence it is crucial to know what you like to do.

2. **Try to experiment with different options**: It takes time to identify your calling or vocation. You can experiment with various options which you enjoy doing or else you can introspect on those activities which give you meaning in your life. This process will help you to choose your calling.

3. **Ask others what they could see you doing:** Many are not clear about selecting their career. When you are confused with so many ideas and thoughts, you can seek help from parents, counsellors, experts, or people who are close to you to get their perspectives about your vocation. They can suggest their viewpoint about your natural talents and virtues.

4. **Follow your heart and intuition:** Many cynics may tell you what you should be doing with your life, or try to demean your dreams and thoughts. You must be smart enough to understand their intent because finding your calling is about being true to yourself and you must take decisions about your call or vocation. Stop thinking about others; what they would be thinking about you; it can curtail your ability to act in your vocation and interests.

5. **Channel your calling into a career:** When you have an idea of your life's purpose, you develop a strategy to put it into action. The eventual goal is to be able to make a living doing what you love. You need not

confine yourself to a single endeavour, if you have diversified interests and expertise.

6. **Pursue your calling as a hobby:** When you cannot put your dreams into action professionally, you can make the room for hobbies you enjoy. Being a teacher, you can write books, publish your articles, conduct coaching for a professional set of skills, you can be a voice artist, etc.

7. **Notice dreams and signs:** All get dreams; however, most ignore them. Write down the dreams that matter to you most. Quite often dreams prompt you to something and show you a direction. Co-relate your dreams with the people you meet, places you visit, the things that happen in your life, etc. You must observe the dreams that matter to you.

8. **Give time for creative expression**: Generally, all discoveries happen through creativity. In today's world when people are engaged in multiple activities and events time has become scarce. Hence you can set aside a few minutes every day to dream about your set of values, your activities, etc.

9. **Be patient**: Refining and discovering your route in life takes its own time. It's a continuous journey. Hence you need to be patient. This will help you to figure out your vocation or calling.

Joseph Irwin Miller, once said, "The calling of the humanities is to make us truly human in the best sense of the word." All are called to grow in grace and knowledge. You mustn't allow others or the world around you to exploit you into their mold but rather allow yourself to grow as per your vocation or calling. People who believe that they have sought a career in response to their call are more satisfied with their career, health, and life

3

DARE TO DREAM

"Every great dream begins with a dreamer. Always remember, you have within you the strength, the patience, and the passion to reach for the stars to change the world."

– Harriet Tubman

"The future belongs to those who believe in the beauty of their dreams,"- Eleanor Roosevelt

At a construction site, John noticed, many people working and he thought of having a conversation with the workers there. He asked one of the workers, "What are you doing?". The worker said, "I am casting cement" He moved around and asked mason the same question, and he replied, "I am preparing the RCC structure" John further moved around and asked the same question, to the contractor, he said, "I am constructing a building."

When John moved further, he found the Project Manager and asked him the same question, he replied, "Sir I am constructing a shopping mall in this upcoming township." Many people are highly confined to matchbox-size dreams, they do not go beyond their regular routines and vacations. On the other hand, there are people who dream always big and also beyond their horizons.

I have a dream; you have a dream, and we all have dreams. Do you recall your childhood dreams? When you were a kid, you might have been enthusiastic to fly an aircraft, aspiring to treat sick people as a doctor, looking for passing orders as a judge, passionate to assemble spare parts as a robotic engineer, zealous to become an entrepreneur or dreamed to buy a seafront house in Juhu or Bandra, etc.

As young kids, there was no limit to our dreams and aspirations. As kids grew into adolescents and adults, they started realizing that most of their dreams and aspirations were unrealistic. Hence many of them changed their dreams to realistic aspects and several others stopped believing their dreams.

Dreams can be accomplished but quite often one has to face obstacles before it becomes a reality. Dreams and aspirations motivate people to look forward to the future. Walt Disney the pioneer of the animation industry, the creator of Micky Mouse, and the founder of Disneyland once said, "If you can dream it, you can do it." He was a great dreamer. He wanted to build a unique theme park that parents and children could enjoy together.

In the early 1950s when Disneyland was in its conception stage, it was considered a massive financial risk and he didn't get the cooperation of other stakeholders of his Company. Despite all the roadblocks, extreme financial risks, and disinterest from other stakeholders, Walt Disney didn't give up. He firmly believed in his dream. He turned to some unorthodox ways to generate revenue to build Disneyland, the most beautiful place on Earth and made it a reality.

David McClelland a Harvard psychologist conducted research on high achievers for more than 20 years and concluded that successful people think, fantasize, and dream constantly about how to improve their performance and achieve their goals. The gateway to becoming successful comes from dreams and aspirations.

Dreams can be spontaneous, or they can be desires that we nurture over a long time. Our dreams are influenced and shaped by what we have seen, read, heard, acted, and admired in our surroundings on regular basis. A former psychologist Aura Sotomayor said, "Dreams give people a major increase in chances for success. One's dreams lead one to their goal. In order to follow one's dreams, one needs to identify the things that may help them achieve that dream quickly and efficiently,"

What is your dream? What does it look like? Are you living your dream now? Or is it something you gave up and feel it is too late to do anything about it? We have grown up with the idea of the ideal age to do something. Every society and culture has its own unwritten timeline for roles, careers, and expertise to be attained. It is a jarring ride if you defy what the majority thinks. It is your life and why worry about what people say?

Anatole France the French poet, journalist, and novelist once said, "To accomplish great things, we must not only act but also dream; not only plan but also believe." Dream, passion, determination, and belief in your abilities can drive you to overcome any obstacle thrown by life.

JK Rowling had to deal with the accumulation of impossibilities in her life. She was broken, clinically depressed, single-handedly had to upbring an infant daughter, and was rejected by atleast 12 publishers. She channeled her privations, misfortunes, and dark thoughts into her writings and ultimately became one of the best-selling authors in history.

There is no fixed rule or fixed age to live your dream. Kimiko Nishimoto is a young at heart Brazilian-born Japanese photographer and internet celebrity. She was previously a hairdresser, track cyclist, and homemaker. She discovered her passion for photography in her late 60s and had a dream to become a photographer. She started as an amateur photographer at the age of 72 after taking a photography and image processing course taught by her eldest son. 10 years later she had a solo exhibition at a Japanese gallery which was a great hit. Her fun quirky portraits are famous worldwide since then.

Many people who initially did something different and outstanding became a hallmark for success and leaders in their field. The followers accepted their qualities as the benchmark for eligibility. If you believe in yourself, you have the power to break the moulds and create new benchmarks.

Dreams and aspirations can also affect people both optimistically, and pessimistically through relationships and experiences. "The Necklace" by Maupassant, Of Mice and Men by John Steinbeck, and "We Choose to go to the Moon" by John F. Kennedy all display dreams that positively or negatively affect relationships and experiences.

Many have dreams and endlessly wait without taking appropriate actions. In fertile soil in a village, there were two wheat grains side by side. The first grain said, "I want to grow! I want to feel the rays of the sun and the dew drops! I dream to bloom in delicate buds and articulate the coming of spring."

It grew up and yielded wheat. The second wheat grain said, "I'm scared. If I grow delicate stems, they can be broken by the wind." It waited for a safer time and one day a passing goose pecked it.

Difference between dreams and goals:

Dreams can continue as sheer wishes if you do not set goals to transform them into reality. It is essential to pursue your dreams with a specific plan of action. The plan of action must be broken into several small goals, which can be achieved.

Goals and dreams look synonymous; however, they are not the same, they are different.

SN	Dreams	Goals
1	Dreams are our wishes and desires we want in life. They are highly subjective and intangible.	Goals are achievable future plans. They are objective in nature and tangible.
2	Dreams are imaginary and they are created in your mind that can take any shape or form.	Goals are something you are acting on. They are specific.
3	Dreams are broad and they don't need focus like goals. You can sit for long hours and dream.	A lot of focus and attention are needed to achieve goals.
4	You can dream something on one day and something else on another.	Goals need to be specific and consistent.
5	There are no deadlines for accomplishing dreams.	Goals are something you actively work on achieving, and there tend to be deadlines associated with them.
6	Dreams require only your imagination in order	Goals, on the other hand, need some sort of investment, time, and

	to be created.	resources.
7	Dreams stretch your imagination driving you to create whatever your mind wants.	Goals stretch your capabilities (character, strength, getting you out of your comfort zone, etc.).
8	Dreams can help you envision a better life for yourself.	Goals can create a change around you and make your dreams a part of your reality.
9	Dreams inspire you.	Goals change your life.
10	The size of success depends on the size of your dream.	Goals are small stepping stones to achieving a big dream.

Dreams need to be nurtured in order to grow, develop, and come true. All must give time to dream. There is a bright possibility that many of you might get busy in your regular routines and sometimes get caught up in unscheduled events, hence you may forget to schedule some time for dreaming or may not get time.

You must try to schedule some time of the day to let your mind wander and dream. As you continue to dream more and more you may become clearer in defining your dreams. Realistic dreams can turn into goals with dedication and perseverance.

4

SET YOUR GOALS

"If you want to be happy set a goal that commands your thoughts, liberates your energy, and inspires your hopes."
-Andrew Carnegie
"All successful people have a goal. No one can get anywhere unless he knows where he wants to go and what he wants to be or do."
— Norman Vincent Peale

"When it is obvious that the goals cannot be reached, don't adjust the goals, adjust the action steps." – Confucius

Bobby Moakley was born deaf. This different ability caused many barriers and hardships in the first 17 years of his life. He felt that he was lagging behind in many areas of life, from friendships to academic achievement. His mindset completely changed once he attended a No Barriers trip through the Grand Canyon.

He studied environmental science at the Rochester Institute of Technology, where he paved the way for many others like him. He was elected Student Government President. He integrated the deaf, hard of Hearing, and hearing cultures on campus. Bobby broke the barriers, accomplishing the most difficult feats by setting goals for himself.

Some people feel as if they are sleepwalking through life with no actual idea of what they need. Possibly they know what they want to accomplish, however, they have no idea how to get there. Many people work hard, but they don't seem to get anywhere valuable. They don't spend enough time thinking about what they want from life and don't set formal goals. Have you seen anyone set on a journey without any destination? Most probably not.

What is Goal Setting?

Goal setting is the first footstep toward planning for the future and plays a vital role in the development of skills from work to relationships. Goal setting is the process of identifying something you want to accomplish with measurable objectives. It can help you in any area of your life, like pursuing your MS from your dream University/College, adopting a healthy and balance diet, getting your dream job, buying a house, etc. When you learn how to set goals in one area of your life, it helps you to set your goals in other areas.

According to the renowned Spanish Painter and Sculptor, Pablo Picasso, "Our goals can only be reached through a vehicle of a plan, in which we must fervently believe, and upon which we must vigorously act. There is no other route to success."

Many get trapped in the cycle of setting goals. They either forget or fail to complete them and set the same goals repeatedly with a renewed resolution to meet those goals. However, these resolutions remain temporary. You must break this cycle with a change of thoughts in your mind. True goal setting requires careful planning, motivation, and discipline.

Goal setting is a skill, and it requires continuous and consistent efforts to learn. Many find it difficult to stick to goals as they don't differentiate them from routine and daily efforts of self-improvement like morning walk, feeding birds, reading newspapers, etc. which are not conscious goals. Goal setting is an overt process of recognizing new objectives you want to achieve, followed by making a plan to complete them.

Why do you need Goal setting?
Setting goals leads to a long-term vision and stresses the acquisition of knowledge and skills. It motivates you to organize your time and your resources effectively and

efficiently. Accomplishing your goals is essential and imperative. However, the most important objective for setting goals is the type of person that you become along the way.

1. **When you set goals, you take control of your work**: The decision-making and action-taking bring you closer to achieving your goals. Industrial-organizational psychologist Edwin Locke found that employees perform better and are further motivated to complete goals if those goals are difficult. In other words, one works less to achieve easier goals.

2. **Setting challenging and achievable goals**: While setting goals you must ask yourself, "What do you want to achieve and what kind of pain are you ready to face?" The actual test is not achieving the goal but rather accepting the challenges and detriments you must undergo in the process of achieving the goals.

   Various studies show that setting challenging and achievable goals increase the prospect of pursuing and fulfilling ambitions. Who doesn't want an award or to win a gold medal? However, very few people want to train themselves like Olympians. Generally, they want instant results with little effort. One cannot choose rewards without remitting the cost. The cost you pay for your goal setting is your time, focused efforts, and patience.

3. **Goal setting directs you to adopt an apt system**: Your goal setting is like the rudder on a ship which determines the direction in which you go, and the

process of the voyage is like the oars that determine the progress. When you are bound to your goal the rudder helps you to move forward. However, if you cartwheel the rudder moves all around, and find yourself moving in circles.

4. **Goal setting stimulates you to eliminate goal competition**: Goal setting helps you to prioritize when you chase multiple goals. In today's demanding world all have multiple goals to achieve within a span of a specific time. Hence your goals are competing with one another for your time and attention. It is essential to pause less important things and focus on a single goal at a time by reshuffling your priorities.

5. **Quite often people tend to set the right goals in the wrong place:** It is difficult to fight your surroundings regularly and achieve your goal as desired. Achieving your goal is strongly influenced by your surroundings and environment. Many find it extremely difficult to stick to positive habits in a negative environment. Hence it is necessary to assess the surroundings and the environment in which you live or work.

If you go to bed keeping your smartphone next to your bed for the morning alarm you will be tempted to access social media, emails, etc. as you wake up, and keep away from your goal of not using the gadgets atleast one hour after waking up or if you are in the company of people who smoke, you will be also likely to catch that habit one day.

6. **Receiving feedback**: Feedback is crucial for achieving your goal. It can be the measuring tool for tracking your progress in achieving your goal. When you measure your progress, you come to know where you stand, and it helps you to learn whether you are spending sufficient time on the things that are important to you.

Types of Goal Setting:

There are three types of goal setting. 1. Process goals, 2. Performance goals 3. Outcome goals

1. **Process goals**: Process goals are definite actions of performing. They are absolutely in control to accomplish. For example, you determine to exercise for 1 hour daily in the evening. It is upto you whether you do it or not.

2. **Performance goals:** Performance goals are grounded on your personal standard. These goals can be mostly under your control, however, there is no absolute control over them. For example, targeting 95% marks in your entrance examination or expecting a job in a premier organization after successfully clearing your tests and interview.

3. **Outcome goals**: Outcome goals are primarily based on gaining, obtaining, or losing. These goals are not in your control. They are regulated by outside factors and influences. For example: Bidding on a tender or expecting a campus placement in a premier corporate with a highly competitive remuneration as you had dreamt.

These three types of goals are linear in their association. When you achieve your process goals, it is easier to achieve your performance goals and when you achieve your performance goals you stand a better chance to achieve your outcome goals.

Skills required for goal setting:
Thomas Edison was a great scientist known for inventing the electric bulb. When his assistant told him in boundless despair and disappointment, "We have failed in 2000 ways in inventing the electric bulb." The optimistic Tomas Edison told him, "We have discovered 2000 ways which are not suitable for inventing the electric bulb." Tomas Edison was committed to his goal and knew the track on which he was going and finally, he invented the electric bulb.

Goal setting is a skill. One must learn and imbibe those skills for efficient goal setting. Some essential skills required for successful goal setting are—1. Planning 2. Self-Motivation 3. Time Management 4. Flexibility 5. Self-regulation 6. Commitment and focus

1. **Planning:** 'Fail to plan, plan to fail' is applicable to goal setting. Planning is fundamental to the practice of goal-setting. It helps to prioritize and sustain focus on the task at hand and avoid distractions.

2. **Self-Motivation:** Self-motivation lit the fire of desire and ambition to achieve a goal. Achieving goals destined to die without self-motivation. It develops new approaches and skills to succeed. It is a powerful benefactor to goal accomplishment.

3. **Time Management:** Time management is a valuable skill in life.   It is mandatory to achieve a goal successfully. Otherwise, your goal is set to fail or become ineffective. It directly impacts the performance of your tasks.

4. **Flexibility:** Flexibility helps you to overcome barriers in your goal setting and achieving your goal. Certainly, sometimes, things don't go as planned. In the face of hardship, it is essential to have the flexibility to help you to reach your goal.

5. **Self-regulation:** Self-regulation stimulates you to regulate and manage your feelings, and emotions in order to achieve your goals. Others cannot control your feelings like anger, fear, overconfidence, bias, etc. you need self-regulate them in order to accomplish your goals.

6. **Commitment and Focus:** You need commitment and focus on your goal setting in order to achieve them.

Principles of goal setting:
Five principles of effective goal setting according to Locke and Dr. Gary Latham:

1. **Clarity**: Goals ought to be defined clearly. When there is no ambiguity in your goals, you know what you're trying to accomplish. Clarity enables you to measure the outcomes accurately and helps you identify the behaviours to reward.

2. **Challenge**: The goals you set need to be challenging to create curiosity and interest. Though people are driven by challenging goals, it's imperative to set goals that are achievable.

3. **Commitment**: You must totally commit to your goals to accomplish them. When your team members are involved in goal setting, they easily understand and agree to the goals. This doesn't mean that you need to secure their approval for every goal. As long as your goals are achievable, they are likely to commit to them.

4. **Feedback**: Regular feedback through assessment and evaluation can reflect tracking of the progress of your goals. Feedback gives you the chance to clarify the expectations of people.

5. **Task complexity**: You must devote time to yourself to reach complex goals. It is essential to ensure that work doesn't become highly overwhelming when goals are exceptionally complex.

What does prevent you from reaching your goal?

Satish was working on an industrial project. All started brilliantly well and he was making good progress. He was excited about future possibilities. However, pride reached his head when the project touched the last stage. He gradually became unmindful of his team and took complete credit for the project at the expense of his team.

In the last stage of his project when Satish started working on certain goals and targets, he didn't get the expected co-operation of his team. Gradually things unraveled, and the set goals took longer time to complete than he thought they would.

Satish lost focus on the goals of his project and started targeting his team on petty issues. He changed some of the team members and hired new ones. The new members came with a new set of ideas and goals for the project. The project continued, nonetheless drifted completely from the original plan. The project didn't meet the expected demands of the industry.

You must work on the following areas to successfully achieve your goal.

1. **Lack of Focus:** Focus is critical when it comes to reaching your goals. When your goals are hazy and not clear you tend to fail to achieve them.

2. **Lack of Understanding:** Some people flip-flop because they fail to understand the process of accomplishing their goals. Many overestimate their abilities and underestimate the difficulties that they are going to face. You also need to understand, how reaching goals will impact your family and friends.

3. **Lack of Planning:** Many people fail to reach their goals due to a lack of planning. Write down your goals, analyze them and make a timeline with different stages of development to achieve them.

4. **Lack of Discipline:** Discipline is crucial in achieving your goal. You need to have a clear and definite action plan. Quite often not following a set plan and discipline is a joy however in the long run it will be a struggle. For example, if you don't feel like waking up early morning and going to the gym or for a brisk walk you will invite illness.

5. **Lack of Hunger:** You need to create a desire and hunger for reaching your goal otherwise, it is going to Fail. You can seek motivation from others who have walked a similar path. Have faith and believe in the goals that you have set to accomplish.

6. **Shiny object syndrome:** Shiny object syndrome is focusing all your attention on something new and trendy at the cost of whatever you are presently doing. It is chasing the latest strategy or tactic which are making the rounds within an industry or in the market. When you are always in pursuit of the next big thing and constantly switching over goals you lose the bigger picture.

7. **Unrealistic or too high Expectations:** Generally, all people have deep desires within and actually want to achieve certain things in life. Nevertheless, many are avaricious and thankless. They expect much more than they deserve even before they receive them.

    Expecting too much is harmful behaviour that brings deep disappointment in your life. When you expect people to behave as you imagine; it can demotivate you to take appropriate action, if it doesn't workout

How to set an Action Plan for your goals?

According to Walt Disney, "A person should set his goals as he can and devote all his energy and talent to getting there. With enough effort, he may achieve it. Or he may find something that is even more rewarding. But in the end, no matter what the outcome, he will know he has been alive."

People, who have determined, and ambitious goals perform better with higher productivity as compared to those who didn't."

Various studies undertaken by research psychologists show, that setting goals drive you to capitalize on the target as if you had already achieved it. Setting goals whether small or big, near or far, the brain believes that the anticipated result is an indispensable part of who you are.

It Sets conditions that motivate you to toil towards the goals to fulfill your self-image in the brain. An action plan is crucial in completing goals as it helps you remain motivated and ensure that you're on track.

1. **Reason for setting goals**: Assess your past goals and reflect on the goals you have set now. The goals which had a definite purpose were successfully achieved, whereas the goals without clear or no purpose weren't successful. Hence always ask 'why' while setting goals for understanding the purpose and relevance of it.

2. **Penning down your goals**: Your action plan must always be put down on paper. It should not remain just

in your mind. When you physically write down your goals you are accessing the logical part of your brain. The goals listed must be specific, measurable, achievable, relevant, and time bound.

3. **Planning the budget and list resources**: All goals do not need funds and a budget, but many do. List down the resources you need to complete your plan and the budget required. Some of the important resources required are time, money, people, and technology.

4. **Listing down the steps for your goals**: Create a step-by-step plan for your goals. List down all the steps or stages including the sub-steps. Ensure the time, budget, and resources required to complete each step of your goals to successfully achieve your goals.

5. **Setting a timeline or schedule**: A set timeline and schedule are essential for completing each step of your goal effectively and efficiently.

6. **Practicing Healthy habits**: Cultivating and practicing healthy habits like following a schedule, appreciating, expressing gratitude, forgiving, being optimistic, motivating, etc. are inevitable for efficiently completing your goals. Negative habits like procrastination, anger, taking credit for everything, etc. can harm in the successful completion of goals.

7. **Conducting Reviews**: Achieving a goal is a process. It cannot be accomplished overnight. In the process of achieving your goals, you may experience various barriers and problems. Hence conducting reviews at regular intervals would help you to track progress and

change some of the objectives that are faulty or not suitable for achieving your goal.

Sample Proforma for Action Plan for Setting Goals

Goal/s	Subgoals	Timeline	Resources

5

BE OPEN TO CHANGE

"I can't change the direction of the wind, but I can adjust my sails to always reach my destination."

– Jimmy Dean

"It is not the strongest or the most intelligent who will survive but those who can best manage change."

– Charles Darwin

"If you always do what you always did, you will always get what you always got." - Anonymous

Vijay was a well-known entrepreneur. He worked tirelessly to build his business empire. He was very clear about his goals in business. Hence, he was successful in all the ventures he undertook. All the employees got their just wages with regular appraisals. The employees worked hard for the growth and development of the company. The assets of the company kept multiplying swiftly. The bond between the employer and employees remained strong. As the business empire grew Vijay gradually changed over to new technologies, practices, and strategies and switched over to a proper management system.

The company gradually changed all its approaches and there was a complete overhaul of the system, practices, and culture of the company. However, the old employees couldn't accept and adapt to changes. They didn't feel at home with the new practices and the new departments. They couldn't approach Vijay directly as used to happen in the past.

As the CEO of the Company one day Vijay ordered formal feedback from the employees for analysis and learned that his old employees were not happy with the changes that happened in the company. After taking the expert advice he adopted a professional model of change management and gradually all the employees got adapted to the new practices and culture of the company.

Change is an inevitable part of life and is crucial for trade, business, or any profession. Change is crucial to its survival like changes in goals, organizational structure, technology, processes, culture, and attitudes. Change occurs as a process, not as an event. Treating change as a process is a central component of successful change and successful change management.

We can easily see change occurring as a process in nature. For example, a monsoon moving into winter or a caterpillar changing into a butterfly. However, changes for individuals when it comes to behaviour and attitude or initiatives for changing the policies in an organization do not happen easily. It requires a proper change management initiative. Change happens when you decide to change, and act on the guiding principles.

Change management is a structured plan to enable individuals, teams, or organizations to transit from an old system to the desired one. It is a designed and vigilant approach to ensure that changes are efficiently implemented for betterment at a personal level or at the level of the organization. Change management focuses on how individuals and teams move to new conditions and adapt to the changes.

Unfortunately, many change initiatives flop because the people in leading positions in those organizations don't adopt change management or a suitable professional model of change management. Change management guides organizations to educate employees to equip them to adapt to changes methodically. It gives a clear purpose and projected results for the greater good. When employees or team members are given time to adapt new strategies, change management provides a bridge to better outcomes.

States of change:

There are three states of change – 1) the current state, 2) the transition state, and 3) the future state which provides a strong framework.

1. **The current state**: The current state is how things are done as of date. It defines who you are or what the systems are. It may not be effective or work great, however, it is familiar and comfortable as people know what is expected of them

2. **The transition state:** The transition state is chaotic and is continuously in flux. It is challenging. The transition state is often emotionally charged—with emotions ranging from fear and despair to anger and relief. Generally, during the transition state, productivity falls. The transition state demands accepting new perceptions and learning new ways while maintaining day-to-day efforts.

3. **The future state**: The future state is where the individual or the organization is trying to get in. Quite often it is not completely defined due to the transition. The future state is expected to be efficient or better than the current state.

Types of change Management for Individuals:

1. Exceptional change management
2. Incremental Change management
3. Pendulum change management
4. Paradigm change management

According to Charles Darwin, "It is not the strongest of the species that survives, nor the most intelligent that survives. It is the one that is most adaptable to change." Change management at the individual level is adopting and engaging through a transition of change. For example, a student admitted to a new school or college, a patient adapting to a new lifestyle after surgery, a government employee switching over to corporate, a bachelor or spinster after marriage, etc. experience drastic changes in life which need to be managed effectively for a fruitful life otherwise it can give major jerks.

1. **Exceptional change management**: When an individual experiences an isolated event in his life and it doesn't move over to other areas of his life, is called exceptional change management.   Its impact is comparatively limited. Example: Due to a traffic jam you reached your office late and couldn't attend the scheduled staff meeting, however, your colleagues gave you the minutes of the meeting.

2. **Incremental Change management**: Solving problems in minor and regular organized phases to drive change over time is called incremental change management. In this category, change is introduced gradually resulting in the complete replacement. Example: Attending regular mindfulness activities improves your mental health, concentration, and empathy, and makes you a good human being.

3. **Pendulum change management**: When one experiences a sudden and complete change. Changes in this category are extreme. Example: During the COVID-19 pandemic you had to switch over to working from home suddenly without any training or preparation.

4. **Paradigm change management**: Paradigm change takes place when practices are integrated into a system which leads to the emergence of a new system. For example: When you started doing your daily exercise, over a period your discipline, health, and lifestyle have been completely changed.

Types of change Management for Organizations:

1. Evolutionary change
2. Revolutionary change
3. Directed or planned change

According to Socrates the famous ancient Greek philosopher, "The secret of change is to focus all of your energy not on fighting the old, but on building the new." Organizational change is a professional prerequisite for development. Attrition, recruitment, creating new departments, adopting new practices, switching over to new technology, etc. lead to a major change in an organization.

It is crucial to keep the employees informed about the changes introduced. They must understand the changes and how they affect them. Change management in organizations is the summation of change experienced by all individuals.

1. **Evolutionary change**: Evolutionary change occurs from natural choice. It is a common type of change experienced by all organizations. It occurs when there are minor changes and a shift in response by a group of people in a changing environment. These changes are not noticed when occurred however reflected later. Example: When HR demands the submission of leave records timely from the employees, the salary roll can be ready on the last working day of the month.

2. **Revolutionary change**: Generally, change occurs when something shakes up the organization and the need for a major overhaul. It can completely change the existing practices, working culture, etc. It creates a major impact on the employees. For example, with the changing demands in the market, employees have to adapt to new trends, the latest approaches, and technology.

3. **Directed or planned change**: Planned change is preparing the whole organization, or an important part of it, for new directions. It can be changes introduced in internal structures, metrics, or dynamics to adapt to innovation, creativity, practices, etc. Example: A firm switching over to a new software through suitable training.

How does change management work?

According to Dr. Martin Luther King Jr. "Change doesn't roll in on the wheels of inevitability but comes through continuous struggle." Change management is primarily the art of managing oneself or others or the organizations during a phase of change. It engages a definite process to support an individual, a team, or an organization to succeed. It ensures getting the right people engaged in the best possible way.

1. **Define the end goal.** Employees and teams need to understand the end goal of any major changes occurring in the workplace or organization. It can get everyone on the same page to effectively adapt to change.

2. **Understand the impact of changes**. It is imperative to understand who is impacted by the change introduced and how it is going to impact them. It may be promotions or new recruitments for a few however for others it may be a radical change in their workflow roadmap. Few may experience small shifts, whereas many others may feel a change in their entire work methods.

3. **Identify key change leaders**. Change leaders can drive change management success. They can boost positivity in their teams and motivate them. The Management must identify different team members who can understand the change and can impact the team in a positive way.

4. **Preparing the teams thrilled about the change**. For a fruitful change, you must bring together those who are impacted. You may also provide different incentives if necessary.

5. **Identifying barriers around change**: Barriers are an integral part of any change. It is necessary to identify the impediments, problems, and difficulties involved in any change for a successful transition. When team leaders work on the barriers team members feel confident to adapt to the change.

6. **Develop effective training**. Training helps employees or teams to successfully adapt to changes introduced in an organization. It drives everyone to understand how the new process works.

7. **Create standard operating procedures**: The management or team leaders need to create standard

operating procedures while implementing changes in an organization to help the employees get used to the change and to provide them with correct information.

8. **Monitor your performance**: Monitoring the changes introduced in an organization is vital for effective implementation. Changes implemented can be monitored through a set of assessment tools, taking regular formal and informal feedback, etc. It helps the team leader or the organization to receive feedback about the changes.

Steps for the change management process:

According to Barak Obama, the former US President, "If you're walking down the right path, and you're willing to keep walking, eventually you will make progress."

1. **Preparing the Organization for Change**: Organizations must be prepared logistically and culturally for implementing any major change to raise awareness of the problems likely to be faced and to avoid resistance and friction from employees.

2. **Crafting a Vision and Plan for Change**: The organizations must create a strong vision and a systematic plan for any changes that are likely to be introduced. A clear vision and an organized plan will enable the organizations to set strategic goals, monitor action plans, measure performance, and strengthen the agility and flexibility of employees and team leaders to beat barriers.

3. **Implementing the Changes**: The plan prepared for the change needs to be implemented step by step that

is outlined. The managers and team leaders must empower their employees and team members to take proactive steps to achieve the goals of the change or initiative. The vision must be frequently communicated to the employees throughout the entire process of implementation.

4. **Grafting Changes in Culture and Practices**: After the complete implementation of the change, the Managers must ensure compliance with the new practices and prevent revision of the old ones. This is necessary for the processes, workflow, strategies, and culture of the organization. An adequate plan will prevent the employees to relapse the revision of the old practices.

5. **Take Feed Back at regular intervals**: Taking feedback at regular intervals is an effective method to measure the progress of the implementation of the change initiative. It offers valuable lessons for future initiatives of change. The feedback needs to be taken from the employees, the change managers, and all the stakeholders of the change initiative. The feedback loop gives the analysis and review of the change initiative and can help Managers and team leaders to understand whether a change initiative was a success, failure, or mixed result.

Change Management is the most challenging facet of leadership. It is essential for leaders to inspire their teams, overcome their confrontation, and build the required impetus that will see them through to success. The need for change is constant. Those who successfully deliver and adopt change will be always in demand. Change management becomes effective when it is interactive and is never done alone.

Today's entrepreneurial activities need agile individuals and organizations. Businesses can survive and flourish only if there is suitable change management. Organizations don't just change merely based on new systems, processes, or structures but also because of the people within the organization adapting and changing. Organizations reap the benefits of change only when the people within the organization make the transition. Hence when the journey of change is made easy the organizations benefit soon.

6

CREATIVITY AND INNOVATION

"Innovation is fostered by information gathered from new connections; from insights gained by journeys into other disciplines or places; from active, collegial networks and fluid, open boundaries. Innovation arises from ongoing circles of exchange, where information is not just accumulated or stored, but created. Knowledge is generated anew from connections that weren't there before."

— Margaret J. Wheatley,

"Creativity is the act of turning new and imaginative ideas into reality. Creativity involves two processes: thinking, then producing. Innovation is the production or implementation of a creative idea. If you have ideas, but don't act on them, you are imaginative but not creative."

—Linda Naiman

There was a unique problem in Japanese grocery stores because of watermelons. The grocery stores were very small and there was no space to waste. The watermelons wasted a lot of space as they were big and round. While trying to find a solution majority of the people responded by saying that watermelons grew round and big. Some suggested if the watermelons were square no space would be wasted, but in reality, watermelons grow round, and nothing could be done about it.

However, some Japanese farmers did not stick to the views of the majority and reality and thought out of the box. They challenged themselves by asking, "If the supermarkets wanted a square watermelon, how can we provide one?"

The farmers thought that the solution to the problem was possible, and they were optimistic about it. They used square boxes while growing watermelons. As the watermelons grew into fruits, they took the shape of a square box. The solution to problem of round watermelons was solved. The farmers found an innovative way of growing square watermelons.

This innovation made the management of grocery stores and supermarkets happy and efficient. It was much easier and more cost-effective to ship the square watermelons. Consumers also loved them because they took up less space in their refrigerators.

The words "Creativity" and "Innovation" are not strange to the modern world. They are frequently used in training sessions, corporate meetings, leadership conclaves, brochures of educational institutions, and Mission Statements of different organizations. In India, we are conditioned to conform from childhood, and any kind of dissent is seen as disrespectful.

To create leaders with vision, creativity, innovation, and problem-solving skills, it is essential to speak up, give contrary views and challenge each other where necessary. The best decisions emerge from spirited debates and discussions. Enterprising and forward-looking classrooms and families promote creativity, innovation, and problem-solving skills.

There is a great pool of talent in creativity and innovation in India, however, it needs a massive push and motivation from policymakers, parents, and educators. It is essential to promote creativity to promote innovation. The innovative scheme Swachh Bharat Swasth Bharat is yielding good results because it is made into a mass movement by the Government of India and equally pushed ahead by all the States and Union Territories; above all people of India have realized its necessity and accepted it as part of their life. It is essential to make creativity and innovation a spirited drive, in school and college curricula in diverse ways.

Quite often people limit their description of creativity to art and to a certain extent to literature. Nevertheless, creativity can come from original thoughts, divergent thinking, problem-solving, inspiration, and imagination in any field.

Creativity is harnessing the power of the mind to conceive new ideas, products, tastes, and sensations, and think of possibilities that no one else has thought of before. It is a form of expression or a technique for solving problems. One can be creative in any context.

Just as there is creativity in art and literature, there is also creativity in sales, marketing, sports, culinary, programming, architecture, medicine, governance, etc. Albert Einstein the great scientist once said, "Creativity is intelligence having fun."

The desi version of Shark Tank was released in December 2021 and aired on Sony Television. The show took everyone by storm across India. We could see entrepreneurs from pan India pitching diverse ideas ranging from detachable sleeves and banana chips to STEM devices and momos.

Some of the stuff was extremely creative. The show made all realize that the common people in India are ambitious and creative and it gave a strong message to the startup ecosystem that creativity and innovation have no limit.

Creativity has no value unless a person makes it a reality or puts it into action. Shawn Hunter, author of Out Think: How Innovative Leaders Drive Exceptional Outcomes, defines creativity as "the capability or act of conceiving something original or unusual" and "Innovation is the implementation or creation of something new that has realized value to others."

Types of Creativity:

Arne Dietrich segments creativity into four types.

1. Deliberate and emotional creativity 2. Deliberate and cognitive creativity	3. Spontaneous and emotional creativity 4. Spontaneous and cognitive creativity

1. **Deliberate and emotional creativity:** People in this category allow their work influenced by their state of emotions. They are sensitive and emotional in nature. They are relatively quiet and take personal time to reflect. They are also logical and rational in decision-making.

   Their creativity is always a balanced product of deliberate emotional thinking and logical actions. This kind of creativity happens to people at random moments. One should find quiet time for deliberate and emotional creativity to happen to them. For example, many authors get the best thoughts for writing their book while traveling or relaxing.

2. **Deliberate and cognitive creativity:** People in this category are purposeful. They are knowledgeable in their field and use their skills and abilities to prepare an action plan to achieve their goal or complete their project. Generally, this type of creativity is developed when people work in a particular field for a long time.

For example, Thomas Edison conducted more than 3000 experiments for inventing the electric light bulb. People in this category spend a lot of time developing new solutions on regular basis. It requires skills, knowledge in a particular field, and dedication.

3. **Spontaneous and emotional creativity:** This type of creativity is found in great artists such as musicians, painters, writers, etc. It is also related to epiphanies. Epiphany is an unexpected awareness of something. This type of creativity is responsible for scientific discoveries or innovations, and philosophical breakthroughs. This drives the person to look at a problem with a deeper viewpoint.

   Spontaneous and emotional creativity does not need specific knowledge to creativity happen but it requires a skill such as writing, musical or artistic. For example, most of the striking dialogues in Bollywood movies directed and produced by David Dawan are created spontaneously in the setting.

4. **Spontaneous and cognitive creativity:** Sometimes people spend a long time finding a solution but without any outcome. However, one day while relaxing in the garden you seem to get a possible solution. The great scientist Isaac Newton got the idea of the law of gravity when an apple fell on his head while he was sitting under a tree and relaxing. Spontaneous and cognitive creativity occurs when one has the knowledge of a particular job however one requires the eureka moment.

Generally, it occurs at the most inconvenient time, such as, when you are relaxing on your bed, taking a shower, enjoying nature's marvels, etc. This type of creativity occurs when one relaxes, the conscious mind stops working and the unconscious mind becomes active. When one involves in lighter, relaxing, and unrelated activities, the unconscious mind connects to the problem one has worked on and provides a solution.

Innovation:

Steven Jeffes, Thought Design Leader, Speaker, and Author said, "Innovation is the unrelenting drive to break the status quo and develop anew where few have dared to go." Innovation addresses the need in society or in the market and creates value. In today's sophisticated world, every organization is looking for innovation for its relevance and survival. Innovation begins with a notion. This notion can be for a new product, service, upgradation in operations, new business model, etc.

Innovations are visible clearly in the form of instruments, physical benefits, or support that solves a problem. They are not only limited to humans but are also possible for various species under diverse conditions and environments. For example, you might have seen in National Geography that monkeys use sticks to pull out food that is kept in unreachable locations or difficult spots. Animals cannot communicate complex ideas, much of what they do is assumed by instinct.

Innovations are necessary for adapting and overcoming the challenges of change. They generate better avenues and are crucial for the survival, economic growth, and success of an organization, firm, or company. Those who innovate are able to set the organization on a new pathway. All can be innovators and all have the ability to innovate. Unfortunately, our curriculum in schools and colleges teaches us about the inventions and innovations of others but doesn't emphasize the innovations and inventions of students in the classroom.

The innovative world encourages creativity and experimentation. Design thinking strikes a balance between the concrete and the abstract. Design thinking is a human-centric and solutions-based, mindset. It's a practical way to strategize and design using insights from observations and research.

In the 1920s, Cadbury's discovered that chocolate was accidentally spilling out of one of its machines, and settling in flaky waves. This led them to develop a series of successful products-Flakes, Twirl, and Snowflake.

Rod wax was an unvalued byproduct of the oil industry. Robert Chesebrough discovered from oil workmen that it could heal cuts and burns. In the 1860s he discovered petroleum jelly and after several years of distilling experiments, in 1870 this product was branded Vaseline Petroleum Jelly. According to the famous English poet William Blake, "What is now proved was once only imagined."

There is one thing in common among today's leaders in business organizations, and that is all of them embrace innovation. Stalwarts like Microsoft, Apple, and Google which have been around for decades or many years owe their continued success to consistent reinvention and innovation. Comparatively new organizations such as Uber and Amazon have dramatically changed the processes at the core of their industries. No organization can expect to maintain an edge if innovation is not part of its strategy.

Creativity Vs Innovation:

The value of creativity and innovation is highly prized in the hi-tech modern workplace. However, many fail to differentiate between these two words. Adam Gutman points out, "Some people think creativity and innovations are synonyms. They are not. Creativity means coming up with a new idea. Innovation is taking this novel idea, and solving customer pain points, and creating value."

Creativity and innovation are related to each other but are separate notions. Both are required for the success of an organization or business. Here's the difference, between creativity and innovation.

SN	Creativity	Innovation
1	Creativity is about coming up with ideas, imaginations, and possibilities.	Innovation is about executing the idea — converting the idea into a successful project or business.
2	Creativity is the capacity to make or think up something uncommon or original.	Innovation is the exercise to create something new which already has a large value to others

3	Generating creativity means allowing people to think outside the box and go against the norm sometimes.	Innovation leads to inventions and growth
4	The quality of thinking about new ideas and putting them into reality is creativity.	The act of executing creative ideas into practice is innovation.
5	Creativity is an imaginative process	Innovation is a productive process.
6	Creativity can never be measured	Innovation can be measured
7	Creativity doesn't carry liability as it is just a thought or idea	Innovation requires money. It can cause liability as the idea becomes reality.
8	There is no risk involved in creativity	Risk is always attached to innovation.
9	Creativity is related to generating new and unique ideas.	Innovation is related to introducing something better into the market.
10	Not every creativity conforms to innovation.	Every innovation is a result of creativity.

How do you promote creativity and innovation?

Pabini Gabriel Petit, the Editor in Chief of UXmatters said,

"Innovation and creativity are the lifeblood of any company that creates products or services," The management of creativity and innovation links the gap between the theory and practice of organizing creativity and innovation. All organizations would like to achieve innovation, however many of them fail to innovate. How can organizations promote creativity and innovation? There are basic techniques and attitudes that can be favourable to generating great and novel ideas.

1. Give Time	3. Encourage Storytelling
2. Give Autonomy	4. Be Consistent

1. **Give Time**: Creativity demands time. Lack of time is the enemy of creativity. Quite often teams in many organizations are constantly busy with an endless backlog of projects to finish. They are stuck churning out tasks and do not have time for new ideas. Any organization or individual looking for innovation or looking for becoming a leader in innovation must set aside time for it. Those who want to innovate must make it a practice of setting aside some time regularly reserved for new ideas and solutions.

2. **Give Autonomy**: The ideas of team members and employees need to be respected and analyzed. If team members are micromanaged, the exercise of setting time for new ideas and innovation will be a waste of time. Organizations that micromanage regular operations suffer from trust deficits and abruptly make changes in certain operations without taking the teams

into confidence. They are scared of experimentation for innovation.

There is no point in setting up exercises that get the creative juices flowing if the organizations do not give freedom or autonomy to team leaders to innovate. Team members influence the output. If they feel ownership of the work or the project it excels or even performs miracles. Team members should be responsible for their decisions and must be guided to build confidence in their work.

3. **Encourage Storytelling**: Content is the key to any work or project or service. It can be branding, communications, marketing, or sales; all need content and not just the central message. The existing processes, methodologies, and guidelines are linear in nature and keep away the professionals from creativity.

   Many organizations work as per the standard procedures and use specific tactics. Standard procedures will not give you creativity and new stories. Teams must be encouraged to try different methods and forget the rules for new stories.

4. **Be Consistent**: There are many organizations that encourage creativity and innovation. However, most of them are not consistent. Organizations can fail despite implementing creativity-boosting actions and innovation if they are not consistent in promoting creativity and innovation.

Quite often many organizations arrange brainstorming sessions for the teams once or twice a year through specialized coaches/trainers. The trainer conducts colourful and brilliant activities, and the participants leave the session with full vigour and energy feeling good about their progress. However, the following day they are back to business as usual. As long as organizations do not set up the next steps after the sessions and assign responsibilities immediately within a few days of the session, it is not going to be useful.

Steven Johnson, Science Author & Media Theorist, said, "If you look at history, innovation doesn't come just from giving people incentives; it comes from creating environments where their ideas can connect."

Running an innovation successfully is altogether different from running smooth day-to-day operations. A successful innovation project needs a great innovative idea, leadership that knows to foster creativity and innovation, the right model, a dedicated team, planning with rigorous experimentation, etc.

Activities like brainstorming, seating arrangement, playing music, conducting team-building exercises, etc. can enable passion among the employees and students and can be useful in encouraging creativity and innovation among them.

It requires making an investment in individuals. However, the management of organizations mostly feels that investment in individuals is not an investment in the organization. Even the most innovative people cannot innovate if they are in an environment that does not sufficiently promote innovation. It is essential to build the right habits to raise the chances of innovation.

Several people feel going to work is an experience they dread. Several organizations fail to create a dynamic culture of engaging the employees or innovative ways of getting done the work, instead they only focus on standardization and routine practices. Though standardization is important innovation and creativity are essential in the workplace. Employees who are encouraged to experiment, explore, and enjoy the work and workplace will be more engaged and come up with creative ideas and better solutions.

What would you notice in a creative and innovative organization?

1. Ideation sessions for employees to openly exchange ideas and problem-solving with colleagues.
2. Inter-functional Teams interacting and collaborating regularly.
3. Leaders utilizing creative activities to stimulate ideas and build cohesion.
4. Arranging, meetings for employees to share thoughts and opinions.
5. Working atmosphere where people can express their own unique style.
6. Flexibility for employees to shape their time and work.

The growth-minded and forward-thinking organizations build a framework within their teams to support consistent creativity and innovation. There are ways to set brilliant thinking into the organizational culture whether it is a social impact organization or a for-profit organization.

7

THE IMPACT OF MINDSET

"Remember that what you are feeling does not reflect your reality! We cannot always control the thoughts that come into our minds, but we can control the thoughts that we dwell on."

-Les Brown

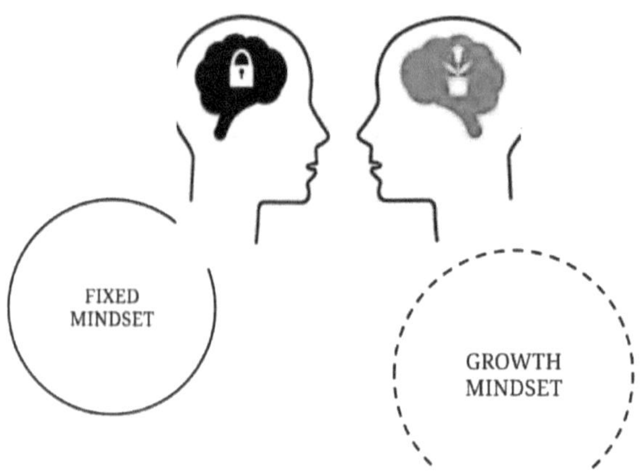

"Think of your mindsets as your foundation. With a solid foundation, you can build something amazing and strong."

Who is not aware of Google? It is a household name across the globe. Google started as an online search firm, now it offers more than 50 Internet services and products. However, do you know about its inception? Larry Page while studying Computer Science at Stanford University, met Sergey Brin and decided to work on a search engine product.

They created a search engine and were struggling to sell this product; no company was ready to buy it. They didn't give up; they furthermore worked hard on the product and launched a company under the name 'Google Inc' in 1998. The product was successful. It was the belief in their abilities and their mindset that made Larry Page and Sergey Brin launch Google Inc.

Why do some people outshine others in any field they select whereas others find it difficult despite having talents and all the advantages? How do people who are successful and skillful get there? Do you consider their success to be the outcome of hard work and, persistent learning from mistakes? or Do you think that they are lucky, gifted, or born talented?

Various studies show that it is the pattern and manner of thinking about one's abilities that matter. Our way of thinking and thinking about our abilities has a direct impact on our achievements and failures at work, in our studies, in relationships, and in our day-to-day activities. Many people fail several times to do certain tasks before they succeed.

However, on the other hand, several others give up when they fail to achieve their goal at a decided time or desired manner. For them, failure is having an obstacle, obtaining low marks, losing a contest, getting fired from a job, having difficult relationships, getting rejected, not doing well in business, and so on.

Success and failure or performance depend on your mindset. For example, the type of mindset Mary Kom and Meerabai Chanu chose in their life made them shine in the Olympics despite their highly marginalized background and unfavourable circumstances. When you have the right mindset, you can conquer any unfavourable situations and backgrounds in life.

According to Stanford psychologist Carol Dweck, "Mindset is something you firmly believe about yourself…Your beliefs play a pivotal role in what you want and whether you achieve it."

Meera and Diksha are twin sisters who passed out from the same college; Meera is heading a team in a corporate and believes that she is an excellent Manager. However, Diksha is still hunting for a job and believes that she doesn't have any skillsets to fit into the job market.

Do you take time to think about the way you think and make assumptions about your mindset and how your mindset can help you to accomplish your goals? Your mindset is a set of beliefs that are influencing how you think, feel and behave in any given circumstance. Some people accept challenges whereas many others evade failures. What you think about yourself, and your abilities determines how you act and lead your life.

Types of Mindsets:

Human behaviour and thinking can be perceived in two ways. 1) Fixed Mindset 2) Growth Mindset.

1. **Fixed Mindset**: The way of thinking that is difficult to change, is known as a fixed mindset. It leads to an intense fear of failure and mistakes. For example, Dinesh feels that he is poor in his public speaking skills, hence he cannot face the audience or speak on the stage.

2. **Growth Mindset**: The other way of thinking that allows you to grow and develop over time, is known as a growth mindset. It encourages you to tackle challenges, passion for learning, and look for greater achievements. For example, Rajesh was shy and had stage fear, however, with his constant efforts he became confident and mastered his public speaking skills.

The Importance of Mindset:

You might have read about a growth mindset and a fixed mindset in various self-help books, and blogs, or heard during various talks and debates. People with fixed mindsets see their qualities are fixed traits that cannot change. People with a growth mindset develop their thinking through efforts, learning, and persistence. Their intelligence, abilities, and thinking lead to a growth mindset.

I recollect the famous fable, 'The Hare and the Tortoise', generally narrated in the Pre-Primary or Primary Classes. This fable is an excellent example of a fixed mindset and a growth mindset. The tortoise takes the challenge and wins the race despite all unfavourable situations and qualities. It stands for growth mindset. On the other hand, the hare was haughty about its speed and fixed mindset which caused it to lose the race despite having all the advantages to win race.

Problems are always opportunities in disguise. People with entrepreneurial mindsets are problem solvers. They identify and resolve problems regardless of the hurdles they face. It is their mindset that drives them to success.

Carol Dweck and her team studied the attitude of students when it comes to failure. After studying their behaviour for a long time, she coined the terms "growth mindset" and "fixed mindset" in her book, Mindset: The New Psychology of Success.

According to Carol Dweck, a mindset is a self-perception that people think about themselves. You may believe that you are smart or not smart or you are good, or you are bad at something. When it comes to your profession you may believe that you are a successful civil engineer or a bad lawyer or a failed professional, etc.

She further adds that many people may be aware or may not be aware of their mindset; yet their mindset can have a deep impact on the acquiring of skills, setting of goals, professional success, relationships, and many other areas of life. Quite often circumstances make many children believe that intelligence is fixed, consequently they avert challenges, hurdles, and even small obstructions.

For example, aspiring entrepreneurs with a growth mindset, make a complete plan, set a brain map of the business, make a budget forecast, and somehow get ready to start their business. Nevertheless, those with a fixed mindset may think that they don't have a background in finance, and relay in their mind fear of losses or thoughts of whether the business would run or not.

The Difference Between Fixed Mindset and Growth Mindset:

The following example gives a brief description of the difference between a fixed mindset and a growth mindset. Michelangelo lived during the Renaissance era and people hailed him as a genius as he sculpted the Pieta at the age of 24.

People had a fixed mindset about Michelangelo; they thought he was born as a sculptor. However, Michelangelo was not on the same page as people thought about him. He said that people didn't know his hard work prior to gaining his mastery and it would not seem so wonderful at all.

He learned how to handle a hammer and chisel from the age of 6 to 10 followed by an apprentice under Ghirlandaio to sketch, copy and prepare frescoes in one of Florence's largest churches. He got trained by the sculptor Bertoldo and other luminaries until the age of seventeen and at the age of 24, he created the Pietà.

Michelangelo believed that talent can be built through perseverance, continuous action, and patience and it can help people to achieve their goals. Michelangelo had a growth mindset.

Fixed Mindset Vs Growth Mindset:

S.N	Fixed mindset	Growth Mindset
1	They avoid challenges	They embrace challenges
2	They feel that talents and abilities are fixed	They believe that talents and abilities can be developed
3	They typically, always focus on the result.	They focus on the process. For them, the process is more important than the result.
4	They run from mistakes and feel that engaging with mistakes will make them look less smart or not smart which is embarrassing.	They try to locate the ambiguities and lacunas and engage deeply in correcting their mistakes. They believe mistakes and errors are part of life.
5	They avoid new initiatives for the fear of failure.	They embrace creativity, innovation, and novelty with the thirst to acquire new skills.
6	They look for people who can praise them and don't like others pointing out their mistakes as they feel they know everything.	They look for people who can challenge them to grow.

7	They feel they are good at something or not good at that.	They know that they can improve their skills.
8	They consider feedback as criticism.	They appreciate criticism as it helps them to learn.
9	They feel that they are already good at something and don't feel the necessity for getting any better.	They know that there are several avenues for learning and that learning is a never-ending process.
10	They feel bad about themselves when they learn about others' successes.	The success of others inspires them.
11	They feel successful people don't fail.	They believe failure is part of success.
12	When they fail, they get frustrated and give up.	When they fail or get frustrated, they keep trying and use the lessons they've learned.
13	They think that one will not fail if one doesn't try.	They believe that one fails if one stops trying.
14	They feel that they are who they are and cannot change.	They believe that they keep changing constantly and progress.

15	They believe if one puts in the excess effort, one doesn't have the ability.	They believe if one put in more effort to challenge themselves, the better they become.

How to change your mindset:

On 10th December 1914, a massive explosion erupted in Thomas Edison's manufacturing and experimental plant at West Orange, New Jersey. 10 buildings comprising more than half of the site were in flames and wiped out. Around 8 fire departments rushed to the scene, but the chemical-fueled blaze was too powerful to be quickly put off.

Tomas Edison's son walked to him as he watched the fire destroying the plant. In a childlike voice, he told his son, "Get your mother and all her friends. They will never see a fire like this again." When his son objected, Thomas said, "It is all right. We have just got rid of a lot of rubbish." **Later, when news reporters asked him about the incident, he told them, "Although I am 67 years old, I'll start all over again tomorrow." As he said, he began rebuilding the next morning without firing any of his employees.**

Neuroscience shows that our brains continue to develop even as adults. It is not only Gen Z who learn the new skill sets but also the analogue generation can immigrate to the newer zones. For that matter, many in Gen Z have a fixed mindset, and several oldies even in their fading years have a growth mindset. Thomas Edison is an excellent example of a growth mindset. Generally, he always responded optimistically to all the circumstances in life.

A growth mindset is not confined to age but to the mind. Our brain is like plastic and can be re-modeled over time creating new neural pathways. It is called neuroplasticity. Mindsets are mere beliefs. Even though they are powerful, they exist only in your mind, and you can change your mind. You have a choice to change your mindset from a fixed to a growth mindset.

Flexibility and broadmindedness are important qualities for a growth mindset. However, these qualities themselves do not qualify you to be a growth-minded person. It is difficult to apply a growth mindset always. Many times, even people with a growth mindset jump to the beliefs of defense mechanisms and fixed mindset while dealing with feelings of insecurity or facing challenging situations or complex conflicts.

Quite often various triggers can activate the dormant fixed mindset; however, they may not remain in that zone for long. It is crucial to identify the reasons for switching over from a growth mindset to a fixed mindset to know whether these triggers are temporary, or they are permanent beliefs.

Strategies to shift fixed mindset to growth mindset:

1. Tell yourself a different story 2. Identify the counter mindset to set learning goals 3. Use your failures	4. Choose the right and realistic tasks for continuous improvement 5. Be consistent and flexible.

1. **Tell yourself a different story:** Words and thoughts have tremendous power. Do your words reflect your thoughts, or is it vice versa? Choose to tell yourself a positive story or thoughts to lift you up. Tell yourself

positive words like you are intelligent to solve problems, or smart to learn new skills, etc.

Nevertheless, the stories and thoughts you tell yourself also must be put into action. The famous German philosopher Ludwig Wittgenstein once said, "The limits of my language mean limits of my world."

When you face hard conflicts or difficult situations, you will respond or react based on your story or thoughts you tell yourself, and in the same manner, you will interpret the conflict or the situation. Your actions are the manifestations of your beliefs. Hence chose appropriate and optimistic words to enable your growth mindset.

2. **Identify the counter mindset to set learning goals:** It is necessary to focus on the process and practice instead of emphasizing only on performance and outcome. For instance, you can eat a healthy and balanced diet and do regular exercise instead of concentrating on losing weight. Focusing on the process can help you learn effectively and reach your goal.

3. **Use your failures:** Failures are the best teachers. One can learn several lessons from failures as compared to successes. All success stories underwent repeated failures in their life. It is evident from the life stories of Dhirubhai Ambani, Narayan Murthy, Sachin Tendulkar, etc.

As you get up when you fall down, so also learn to rise when you fail. You can apply various mental models to create new strategies and take guidance from others to review your decisions. When you prepare your mind to look at failures as a tool for learning, you will grow.

4. **Choose the right and realistic tasks for continuous improvement:** Growth-minded people embrace challenges. However, embracing challenges doesn't mean that you have to aim at doing something unrealistic or impractical.

   For example, aiming to win an Olympic medal in athletics at the age of 35 with little practice and preparation or aspiring to become a civil engineer without taking Mathematics are not realistic. You must choose the right and realistic tasks as challenges like goldilocks' tasks. This will help you to set up a path for continuous learning and gradually build your abilities.

5. **Be consistent and flexible:** Shifting from a fixed mindset to a growth mindset doesn't take place overnight. What works for one person may not work for another. It requires consistent efforts and practice and requires flexibility to change your mind from one zone to another.

People are capable of changing their brain functions and their thinking pattern. Whatever you want to accomplish, you must always combat negative self-talk that attempts to persuade you that you are going to fail. Once your mindset changes, everything on the outside will change along with it.

You must be ready to fail sometimes and take responsibility for it, by accepting failure as a test or an avenue instead of accepting defeat. Your actions come true as per your mindset. Optimism leads to a mindset of confidence, and determination and helps you to overcome challenges. A growth mindset is a maker of great character.

MIRACLES OF MOTIVATION

"The most important thing changing human behaviour is the person's motivation."

"Motivation awakens excitement, happiness, positive expectations, and positive energy."

Sanchit was a career-minded guy. He always looked for better opportunities in his career. He used to assess any organization only from the package of remuneration. When Sanchit reached his mid-thirties, he was financially sound, socially well-respected in his industry, and well-settled in life. He got sound remuneration from whichever organizations he worked for, and the high pay packages motivated him to work for the organizations he served. However, he was not happy within. He never got job satisfaction in the organizations he worked for.

One day Sanchit accidentally happened to meet Rachit one of his old college friends in an Industrial Conclave. They had a lengthy discussion after the conclave. Sanchit learned that Rachit has been working for only one organization since he got placement at his college campus. Rachit was very happy with the organization and his organization had sound employee policies and schemes which motivated him to stick to the organization. Rachit was financially not as sound as Sanchit, however, his high job satisfaction and the organization's employee welfare policies made him stick to the same organization.

What drives you to work or complete an assignment? How do you achieve your goals? What makes businesses successful? Why do we care about what people want and why they want it? Why do employees do what they are asked to do? Many might say the answer to these questions is efficient management. However, there is something more than efficiency that makes the employees do their job or make the businesses successful. There is some power within that drives you to do your work or achieve your goals. It is also true when it comes to relationships. That power is called motivation.

Motivation is the driving force behind everything you do in your day-to-day life. It is the stimulus to act or move. It is a spark that boosts your feeling, thinking, behavior, and energy. It is a power that drives you closer to your dream and leads you to acquire cherished outcomes like personal growth, better well-being, improved performance, or a sense of confidence. Motivation works like glucose which gives energy and shows you a purpose to live. Everyone needs the motivation to achieve their dreams and aspirations.

It is the motivation that makes students work hard in their studies so that they can build the career of their interest. It is the motivation that makes sportspersons struggle hard to win medals in national or international level events. It is the spark of motivation that impelled Steve Jobs to launch Apple; iPhone and iPad are the results of his passion and motivation.

Many people lack belief in themselves and are often in denial of their own abilities. They quite often land up saying, "I can't do that" or "I am not prepared". Your life can be dull without a spark. One must stay motivated to gain confidence or to achieve what one wants in life.

Importance of motivation:
Motivation is the fuel that drives the achievement of every goal. Without motivation, it is difficult to accomplish goals. In an organization, motivation is the process of persuading

employees to act in a desired manner to achieve organizational goals. If you study motivation you come to know significant insights about human nature.

It describes setting goals, striving for achievement and power, desire for love and intimacy, the experience of fear, anger, empathy, etc. When you study motivation, you come to know where it comes from, why it changes, what facets of it cannot be changed, why some types of motivation are more useful than others, etc.

Increased motivation has many benefits. It energizes our relationships, our work, our health, the functioning of our well-being, and so on. Qualitative motivation allows you to thrive. It is noticeable in student engagement, job satisfaction among employees, flourishing relationships, etc. Fluctuations in motivation affect people drastically. However, unhealthy variations in motivation can lead to addiction, gambling, etc. It is challenging and difficult to change the behaviours of those who are involved in situations of addiction. Example: Addiction to social media, substance use, etc.

Motivation can create both desirable and undesirable changes among people. It varies from person to person and from one situation to another. Despite giving incentives some are disinclined to change, few are unable to change, and many others are not fully ready to change. Motivation is a significant facet of management. A motivated employee is an asset to an organization or a team.

According to Blaise Pascal, a French mathematician, physicist, inventor, philosopher, writer, and theologian "People are better persuaded by the reasons they themselves discovered than those that come into the minds of others." Motivation controls human behaviour sets the direction for actions, and is consistency. It is influenced by culture, society, education, and lifestyle. All cultures have their own motivation drivers. Your motivation is also determined by the culture and values you were brought up.

A child who is brought up in a family where religious harmony is respected learns to respect other religions and will be motivated to take up inter-religious dialogue. Some are highly influenced by the social groups with which they are associated. If your groups contain many people who place priority on professional competence and achieving professional success, you will be motivated to strive for promotions because of your surroundings.

Types of Motivation

Broadly speaking there are two types of motivations

1. Extrinsic Motivation
2. Intrinsic Motivation

Extrinsic motivation:

Extrinsic motivation denotes behaviour determined by outside factors/rewards. It can be concrete rewards like salary increments, or abstract rewards like admiration. Extrinsic motivation is classified into two- a) Compensation   b) Punishment

    a. **Compensation**: Compensation can be bonuses, appraisals, etc.   This motivation drives the employees to come on time, complete the tasks assigned as scheduled, and so on. A Retail Market

Outlet was incurring losses. The Manager of the Retail Shop Outlet decided to motivate the salespersons by promising to give them a bonus if they achieved their month's target. The sales team achieved their target much before the end of the month. Reward in the form of compensation always motivates employees.

b. **Punishment**: Punishment can be charging of fine, issuing a memo, etc. Generally, punishment as motivation is mistakenly taken as negative, however, its intentions are positive. Example: The fear of punishment makes people follow traffic rules. Ashok used to regularly reach late to his office. He was given multiple warnings followed by a few memos. One day the Manager warned Ashok that if he came late again, he would be fired. Ashok realized the necessity of his job and started reaching his office on time.

Intrinsic Motivation:

Intrinsic motivation drives a person to be rewarded internally. It gives them inherent satisfaction. An intrinsically motivated person is driven by fun or challenge. According to Dennis Coon, author of 'Introduction to Psychology: Gateways to Mind and Behavior With Concept Maps', "Intrinsic motivation occurs when we act without any obvious external rewards. We simply enjoy an activity or see it as an opportunity to explore, learn, and actualize our potentials."

Example: Many people participate in sports events like marathons for fun rather than to win a medal or reward.

People participate in many activities daily driven by intrinsic motivation. It could be going for a brisk walk, learning a new set of skills, helping the needy, etc. It gives them a sense of satisfaction to live a fulfilled life. All relationships work with intrinsic motivation.

Intrinsic motivation can be classified into 4 categories

1. Creative Motivation
2. Competence Motivation
3. Learning/Exploring Motivation
4. Attitude Motivation

Creative Motivation: Creative motivation is a persuasive internal feeling. Creative people are motivated to express their ideas which are in their mind and heart. For instance, it can be writing stories/poems/novels, painting sceneries, starting a business, learning musical instruments, composing music, etc.

Kartik was an excellent computer engineer from the Indian Institute of Technology and was equally gifted in his creative skill of writing stories. He was serving in a multinational company and was well settled in life. Occasionally he used to publish his stories in national magazines. He did it as a hobby and not for moncy.

The readers loved the genre of his stories, hence the publication requested Kartik to publish his stories more often. Readers liking for his stories motivated him to write furthermore creative stories. Over time Kartic was well known as a brilliant writer and less known as an excellent computer engineer.

Competence Motivation: Success can drive the overall growth of one's competence. A sense of competence can bring great self-motivation. It makes people upskill in their field or profession for development and growth. Competence motivation makes people compete with their teammates or peers to do better. It gives them a sense of satisfaction.

Arnav is a young basketball player. He loves playing basketball; however, he is not as competent as other players. All players practice for training for two hours a day at the court, however, Arnav spends another extra hour at the court for more practice. Arnav's passion for basketball motivates him to spend an extra hour to better himself in the game and not for praise.

Learning/Exploring Motivation: Learning is a continuous and never-ending process. Learning motivation makes people explore, experiment, and learn to achieve their goals. The desire to learn is an excellent intrinsic motivation in people. It makes people innovate, explore new ideas, and look for new perspectives.

Laxmi was obese and had various health issues. Despite knowing the fact that she was not feeling healthy she could not maintain a routine of exercise and discipline of eating healthy. Many tried to guide her to maintain good health but somehow were not successful. One day she was persuaded to attend a session on Good Health and Fitness which made her change her lifestyle and eating habits.

She joined the yoga asana classes. Initially, she struggled to do the asanas, but though it was difficult she kept trying. As she continued with regular exercise, healthy eating habits, and a healthy routine, she began feeling better and felt more energy in her. Gaining good health motivated her to follow discipline in her lifestyle. With her continuous efforts and hard work, she took control of her health. Over time she herself became a Fitness Coach motivating other people to maintain good health and fitness.

Attitude Motivation: 'Attitude Motivation' drives you to make people around you feel good and it brings joy. It is inclined towards bringing positive change in people and motivates you to do more. Sheela loved stray cats and dogs and fed them quite often. Somehow, she was not satisfied with her work. She always felt sad about homeless dogs and cats and wanted to rehabilitate them. Sheela set up a programme to rehabilitate stray dogs and cats and find foster homes for them. Her work didn't fetch her money, but she felt good about her work.

Difference between intrinsic and extrinsic motivation

SN	Intrinsic motivation	Extrinsic motivation
1	Drives from inside	Derives from external factors
2	Difficult to kindle	Easily boosts with reward
3	Difficult to apply to a group	Easily can be applied to a group
4	Performance is driven from within	Performance is persuaded by external factors such as rewards or punishments,
5	There is no reward or pressure to perform	Performance enhances through factors of motivation like rewards or punishment
6	Fostering intrinsic	It occurs instantly based

	motivation is a long process,	on the reward or punishment.
7	It lasts for longer and leads to a higher level of performance. Example: Rajesh goes for regular football coaching because of his interest in football. The game motivates Rahesh to attend regular coaching classes.	It generally occurs for a limited period of time. People become dull once the reward is given. Example: Suresh is told by his father that he would be given a new bicycle if he attends regular football coaching. Reward motivated Suresh to attend the football coaching classes, however, after getting the bicycle, his interest in the coaching classes gradually declined.

THE POWER OF POSITIVE THINKING

"The positive thinker sees the invisible, feels the intangible, and achieves the impossible."

\- Winston Churchill

"Keep my word positive. Words become my behaviors. Keep my behaviors positive. Behaviors become my habits. Keep my habits positive. Habits become my values. Keep my values positive. Values become my destiny."

\- Mahatma Gandhi

"One positive thought produces millions of positive vibrations." —John Coltrane

In a small town lived a boy named Shekhar. He started working as a labourer to support his family after passing out in distinction in class XII. His ambition in life was to become an IPS Officer and serve society; he was hopeful about it. After working for a year, he continued his studies in an evening college. However, the contractor and the site supervisor discouraged him to continue his studies.

Even his fellow labourers mocked him about his dreams and they felt Shekhar was unrealistic. His hope and positive attitude facilitated him to keep the fire lit to complete his studies despite all the harassment and dissuasion in his life. His hard work, belief in his abilities, and positive thinking helped him to overcome all the roadblocks in life. As a result, one day he becomes an IPS Officer.

Positive thinking is the key to a happy and successful life. It drives the progress of virtues within us. Our mind is a powerful tool that generates thoughts. Thoughts are generated when we are awake or asleep through our conscious or subconscious minds.

Our thoughts create energy. It can create heaven out of hell or hell out of heaven. It depends on how you tackle your thoughts. Thoughts never stop and they play an important role in your personality. Our habits are created from our thought processes. What we frequently think we become.

Who doesn't want to be happy and successful in life? We need to master what to think and what not to think more than anything else. Your thinking can make you content or dejected. That is why you need to focus on learning the art of thinking. The approach of positive thinking creates a more positive experience in life.

Daksh considered himself a failure and saw a problem in every opportunity. Once he applied for a new job and subsequently, he was called for an interview. However, Daksh was apprehensive about his selection, and various types of negative thoughts circulated in his mind. He thought to himself that other candidates were far better than he was.

On the day of the interview, Daksh felt feverish. He could not focus on the interview. His negative thoughts invited all types of distractions and hence he couldn't clear his job interview despite having the necessary skills and competence.

On the other hand, Jatin too was called for the same interview, and he too was not selected for the job. However, Jatin was confident and believed in his abilities. He always saw a silver lining in every problem. When someone asked him, whether he was selected for the job, he responded by saying that he was waiting for better opportunities. Jatin worked on improvising his existing skills and later he was recruited by a multinational organization with far better remuneration and facilities.

Both Daksh and Jatin faced the same interview, and both were not selected, however, they had a different outlook on life. Daksh's thoughts drained his energy, whereas Jatin's thoughts boosted his power of thinking. People with positive thinking are confident and believe that they can overcome any obstacle or difficulty they face. To achieve positive thinking and sustain it you need to practice it.

Norman Vincent Peale in his book, 'The Power of Positive Thinking,' popularized the concept of positive thinking and provided practical instructions to achieve an optimistic attitude in life through affirmations and visualizations. Visualize useful situations and avoid imagining negative thoughts to attract positive energy when you do any work or in your relationships.

According to Mahatma Gandhi, "Keep your thoughts positive because your thoughts become your words." Use positive words in your conversation and in your inner dialogues such as I can, I am able, etc. Frequently repeating positive affirmations will help you reduce your self-limiting beliefs and can boost your morale when you do any work, undertake any project, or in your relationships.

It does not mean that positive thinking will cast away all your problems or lead you only to success. Mere positive thoughts are not sufficient, they must be accompanied by action in the right direction. According to Grant Fairly, a motivational speaker, and coach, "A positive attitude may not solve every problem, but it makes solving any problem a more pleasant experience."

Quite often it is very difficult to feel positive when you are grieving or experiencing some serious distress. However, positive thinking will give you an optimistic way of looking at problems, facing various challenges, tackling critical issues, and helping you to work towards solutions in a productive way. It is important to find a silver lining to channel positive energy in such circumstances. Positive thinking helps you to move ahead.

According to Helen Keller, "Keep your face to the sunshine and you cannot see a shadow." Positive thinking is not about concealing negative thoughts or emotions or evading complex feelings. When you have a positive state of mind, you are better equipped to cope with stress, and hardships, develop tolerance, think more creatively, and tackle solving problems effectively.

Raji had a pet rabbit. He loved it more than anything else. Both Raji and the pet rabbit used to spend time daily caressing and conversing with each other. One day as the rabbit was in the garden, it picked a flower to hand over to Raji. As the rabbit handed over the flower to Raji it said, "I picked this flower for you, but I forgot and ate the top."

Raji smilingly looked at the rabbit and fondly said, "That's ok, love doesn't have to be perfect. It just needs to be real." This gesture of the rabbit indicates a sign of a positive environment in which both Raji and the rabbit lived.

According to Swami Vivekananda, "We are responsible for what we are, and whatever we wish ourselves to be, we have the power to make ourselves." Positive thinking means you look for solutions and expect to find them. Problems should not be ignored but rather you should take responsibility consistently.

Positive thinking enables you to accept challenges and makes you work to find a solution. A positive attitude leads to an optimistic outlook and hope. You will believe things will work out well and you find success.

Developing a positive attitude and positive thinking is like a butterfly effect. It can help you in numerous ways that you might not realize and can help you in more ways than you might realize. When you think something positive your subconscious mind does not allow negative thoughts to creep in.

According to Winston Churchill, "POSITIVE: The positive thinker sees the invisible, feels the intangible, and achieves the impossible." Creating positive thinking and attitude requires effort and it must be learned. It must be a continuous process, and it must be practiced to acquire amazing results. After you learn how to think positively, you will notice amazing changes all around you. Your brain will begin to operate feel-good hormones called endorphins, which will make you feel lighter and happier.

Find ways to thank others for the help they render in one way or the other to make you feel happy. People acknowledge the goodness in their lives with gratitude. Practicing gratitude can perform miracles in your mind and heart. It can reduce stress, improvise self-esteem, etc. Expressing gratitude generates positive emotions, delights good experiences, boosts health, tackles adversity, shapes strong relationships, and makes you feel and think positively in life.

Demi Lovato once said, "No matter what you're going through, there's a light at the end of the tunnel and it may seem hard to get to it but you can do it and just keep working towards it and you'll find the positive side of things."

Positive thinking is keeping an optimistic mindset even when things are in absolute disarray. What a balanced diet does to your body, positive thinking does to your mind. Serving your mind with positive thoughts will create amazing changes around you.

The journey to success commences with a positive mindset. Positive thinking helps you to develop a growth mindset. Positive thinkers are optimistic, and they know how to keep negative thoughts away and help others to see the world in a new light. They don't blame themselves or others when things go wrong. They are in total control of their emotions and seek valuable lessons in every setback they experience.

10

MAGNETISM OF LEADERSHIP

"Good leaders build products. Great leaders build cultures. Good leaders deliver results. Great leaders develop people. Good leaders have a vision. Great leaders have values. Good leaders are role models at work. Great leaders are role models in life."

—Adam Grant,

"The greatest leader is not necessarily the one who does the greatest things. He is the one that gets the people to do the greatest things."- Ronald Reagan

The skein of geese flies in a "V" formation when they migrate in the winter. As each goose flaps its wings, it creates an upthrust for the goose immediately following. When they fly in a "V" formation, the whole skein of geese adds a far greater flying range than if each goose flew on its own. If a goose falls out of the formation, it suddenly feels the drag and resistance of trying to go it alone and quickly gets back into the formation to take benefit of the lifting power of the goose in front.

When the goose on the lead gets tired, it moves back, and another goose takes the lead. At the same time skein of other geese honk from behind to boost up those in front to keep up their speed. If a goose gets sick or is wounded by a gunshot, and falls out of formation, two other geese fall out with that goose and follow it down to give support and protection. They stay with the fallen goose until it recovers and is able to fly or until it dies, and only then they do launch out on their own, or with another formation to catch up with their group.

Did you ever feel that you were called to do something? We are called to influence people around us and make a difference in their life. It is called leadership. Leadership is the ability to persuade and guide the people/employees/followers of an organization, religion, political party, etc. Anyone who can motivate others to follow them is a leader.

Leadership is not confined merely to position or chair; it happens at all levels. It can mean different things to different people and in different situations. Effective leadership sets direction creates a vision and adapts to circumstances. Basically, leadership is eliminating hurdles so that people can act or execute their work without hindrance, and it stimulates action from followers, workers, team members, etc.

Winston Churchill is remembered as one of the greatest leaders in modern history who led Britain and the Allied powers to victory against the Nazis during the Second World war. His wisdom, upright character, and determination led Britain from the brink of defeat to victory. He was not only instrumental in working with the USA and USSR to defeat the Axis powers but also in establishing peace, post-Second World War.

According to Michael Useem, a management professor, "Leadership is most effective when it also comes from below. And in today's complex, globalized workplaces, leadership often comes from many directions." Leadership is an essential management function to help an organization, association, or team to direct its goal accomplishment and efficacy.

Leadership is a crucial element for making an organization successful. Good leadership is indispensable to industries, business organizations, political parties, religions, and all segments of society. In today's world leadership is not a solitary activity. Distributed leadership is increasingly well known today as it is suitable not only for large and complex organizations but also for smaller ones. Organizations that develop leaders achieve excellence.

What makes a good leader?

Gen. Colin Powell, former U.S. Secretary of State once said, 'Great leaders are almost always great simplifiers, who can cut through argument, debate and doubt to offer a solution everybody can understand." Oprah Winfrey an author, talk show host, philanthropist, and billionaire is a successful celebrity well-known for talk shows. However, she grew up in poverty and struggled with financial problems, domestic issues, and situations of abuse. She was privileged to get a support program at her school which helped her to opt for a better high school with better prospects for education. After winning a local beauty pageant, she took up a part-time job with a news agency in Nashville. It was there she discovered her liking for media.

Oprah built a successful career in media. She hosted unique and innovative programmes. Her television show lent an emotional-centric approach. She hosted guests to hold discussions on their personal confessions, self-help ideas, and techniques for conquering adversity. She earned millions of fans due to her charismatic personality and her compassionate approach. Her fanbase looked to her for help and emotional support in their challenges and crisis.

Leaders create a vision for the organization, team, followers, or party. A vision provides direction, makes priorities transparent, and drives to create a roadmap to success. Leadership embodies the vision in everything they do and links it to the performance of followers or employees to make it a reality. Good leaders create a vision for the future, work successfully with the team, establish flexibility, take lead, and promote the success of the team. The skill required to bring these traits together in a person or a group of people is called leadership.

Leadership looks into how their organization or industry is going to evolve and how their competitors are going to respond to their initiatives. They test their vision with the stakeholders and assess the risks and benefits. Leaders are proactive in solving problems and look ahead of time. They show the projected future of the organization and tell inspiring stories to explain their vision to make it meaningful to the people they lead.

Good leaders make sound and challenging decisions establish realistic goals and build a roadmap for the followers to achieve the goals. They are confident, charismatic, strong in communication and management skills, possess creative and innovative thinking, persevere in the face of failure, are willing to take risks, are open to change, and are resilient in times of emergency or crisis.

Some noteworthy individuals who have exhibited exceptional leadership in their respective fields are- The Iron Man of India Sardar Vallabh Bhai Patel, "The Saint of the Gutters" Mother Theresa, the co-founder of Apple Steve Jobs, etc.

1. The Iron Man of India Sardar Vallabh Bhai Patel integrated 562 states into the Union of India in 1947 and 1948 through his vision, tact, diplomacy, and pragmatic approach. His strategies, tactics, and leadership prevented the Balkanization of India. We the citizens of India owe an immeasurable debt of

gratitude to the Architect of Modern India for his invaluable contribution to nation-building.

2. Mother Theresa well known as "The Saint of the Gutters" started her journey living among the poor in the slums of Calcutta. She went door to door, begging for food and financial help. She survived on the bare minimum and used the excess to help the poor. She nursed the dying on the streets, served the destitute, treated the lepers, and so on. Eventually, her selfless efforts were recognized, and started receiving support from various sources.

She spread her service not only across India but also across the globe. When she died on 5th September 1997 her service was spread to 125 countries across the globe with 605 homes to serve the destitute. Today her congregation is spread in 140 countries with 745 homes continuing her mission. It was Mother Teresa's clear vision, exceptional mission, strong leadership, and love for the poor that made her a living legend.

3. Steve Jobs was the co-founder of Apple. He started Apple in 1976 in his parent's garage. He was expelled from Apple in 1985 and returned to save it from bankruptcy in 1997. When he died, in October 2011, he had built the empire of Apple into the world's most treasured company.

At the same time, he facilitated the transformation of seven other industries: personal computing, animated movies, music, phones, tablet computing, retail stores, and digital publishing. He is thus added to the list of

America's great innovators, along with Thomas Edison, Henry Ford, and Walt Disney.

Dana Brownlee the founder of Professionalism Matters once said, "I think a great leader is one who makes those around them better. There are many litmus tests for a great leader, but I really look to those around them: Are they growing, becoming better leaders themselves, motivated, etc.?"

Leaders must be aware of their own motivations, abilities, and shortcomings to be effective leaders. Good leaders connect with their teams by facilitating open communication, encouraging employee growth and development, and giving and receiving feedback.

Leadership is a process; it takes time to hone and comes through experience. One cannot become a good leader merely by browsing qualities through search engines or merely sitting on the chair and issuing orders, or merely reporting the higher up. One must understand & follow the vision & mission of the organization, learn management skills followed by great leaders, read books on self-development and leadership, conduct SWOT (Strength, Weakness, Opportunities & Threats) analysis, and be sensitive to the needs of the people they serve or people in their team.

Good leadership is creating an optimistic impact on the team members and also on the organization. Employees under good leadership tend to be happier, more productive, and more connected to their organization. It creates a ripple effect. Leaders with integrity, critical thinking, realistic goal setting, positive reinforcement, building relationships, transparency, etc. can build effective teams for the success of an organization or society.

Managers as leaders:

The success of any organization is based on the leadership of managers. There is a difference between a manager and a leader. All leaders are managers, but all managers are not leaders. Progressive organizations encourage their managers to be leaders who could influence the employees for the betterment of their organization.

Quite often Managers do not play the role of a leader. They remain mechanical in their role and robotic in their response. A manager must be a leader who makes an organization flourish and keeps the employees together. They must be effective, and persuasive in creating an environment, and in achieving overall goals and better results.

Leaders Vs Managers:

SN	Leaders	Managers
1	Leaders lead a team and influence the team members to perform and achieve the goals.	Managers manage an organization or a project or a team giving direction and keeping control of achieving the goals.
2	They are transformational in their process of achieving goals	They are transactional in the process of doing a project.

3	They are strategic thinkers, open-minded, promote innovation and exhibit team management.	They are tactical thinkers, give orders, and conform to standardization.
4	They create a surrounding of influence and inspiration.	They create a power center and lead by authority.
5	They look after a team	They supervise a team
6	They shape the culture and drive integrity.	They conform to the existing culture.
7	They set directions to achieve a goal.	They set instructions to do a project or task.
8	They promote change, take risks and accept challenges and use conflict as an asset.	They react to change and suppress conflict.
9	They always say 'We" while giving directions to the team members or subordinates.	They always say "I" while giving orders to the team members or subordinates.
10	They know how work is done and encourage team members to get it done better or do it differently if it is more effective.	They show how work is done and ask the team members to follow the orders.

11	They focus on relationships and objectives	They focus only on objectives
12	They command informal authority by virtue of personal qualities	They show formal authority due to the position they enjoy.
13	They follow both formal and informal structures	They follow only formal structures
14	They are foresighted and far-sighted	They don't look beyond the decisions or policies.
15	They are both people and process-centric	They are only process-centric
16	They look for effectiveness	They look for efficiency

Leadership styles

Leadership style plays an important role in the success of any organization. The leadership style denotes the qualities and characteristic behaviours of a leader. Good leaders create social change. Many leaders have a dominant style while some use different styles in different situations or with different teams.

Effective leaders are able to shift their leadership approach based on the goals or situations. Hence many organizations look for leadership skills in the list of competencies while recruiting managers. There are several leadership styles that can be leveraged in various circumstances to achieve results.

The 5 most common leadership styles are:

1. Transformational Leadership.	4. Transactional Leadership.
2. Delegative Leadership.	5. Participative Leadership.
3. Authoritative Leadership	6. Affiliative Style

1. **Transformational leadership**: Transformational leaders encourage, inspire and motivate employees to innovate and generate change that will nurture and shape the future success of the organization. They motivate their workforce without micromanaging. They entrust trained employees to take charge of their allocated jobs.

   For example, Elon Musk's leadership style is transformational and focuses on creating real positive change in the world. Transformational leadership encourages employees to be more creative, look to the future and find new solutions to old problems. Employees are also prepared to become transformational leaders themselves through mentorship and training.

2. **Delegative Leadership**: Delegative leadership is often referred to as "laissez-faire". Leaders in delegative leadership focus on delegating initiatives to the team members and they allow their team members to direct their own decision-making. Employees in

delegative leadership find a sense of independence which empowers them to develop their problem-solving skills by finding solutions appropriate to situations.

For example, Warren Buffet an American business magnet, investor, philanthropist, and the Chairman & CEO of Berkshire Hathway, allows his employees to take responsibility for their actions and decisions. When he invests in a company, he does not interfere in its operational or strategic decision-making.

3. **Authoritative Leadership**: Authoritative leaders are in complete control. They set goals, determine the processes, and oversee all the steps to achieve the goals with little input from team members. They drive the organization towards common goals. They work with employees at every step of their processes, leading and coaching them to success.

This type of leadership is effective for urgent needs and emergencies where an immediate solution is necessary or indispensable. This type of leadership can boost productivity just before deadlines and it improves decision-making during times of crisis or challenges. This style of leadership works well where there is little room open for errors.

4. **Transactional   Leadership**: Transactional leaders focus on results and conform to the existing structure of an organization. They measure results as per the organization's system of rewards and

penalties to achieve optimal job performance from the employees.

Transactional leaders have formal authority and positions of responsibility in an organization. The manager rewards team members who execute their tasks to the specified echelons and take to task those members who do not perform as per the set standards.

Transactional leadership is effective in accomplishing short-term goals quickly. It is effective in a structured environment where there are few deviations from established processes and defined roles. Generally, employees under such a setup are not self-motivated. They are mostly motivated through reward and punishment.

5. **Participative leadership**: Participative leadership is also known as democratic leadership. In participative leadership members of an organization work together to make decisions. Managers listen to their team members and involve them in the decision-making process.

    Participative leadership is not common in the corporate world. However, some professions require this approach most of the time and while many others require it in many situations.

6. **Affiliative Style**: Affiliative leaders adopt a "people-first" approach and try to create and sustain a peaceful

work environment. As compared to other leadership styles, leaders in the affiliate style get very close to the team members or employees. In the affiliative leadership style, the leader pays attention to the employees and supports the emotional needs of the team members.

Affiliative leadership focuses on building team bonds, and emotional connections, and resolving any team conflicts. Affiliative leadership can be very helpful when a new team is forming or when an existing team is in turmoil requiring emotional support.

Affiliative leadership must be used carefully as it can be counterproductive while building relationships. This leadership style must be used as per the circumstances in select situations, otherwise, it can also lead to a loss of focus on the true goals of the organization.

According to Chris Hadfield, "Ultimately, leadership is not about glorious crowning acts. It's about keeping your team focused on a goal and motivated to do their best to achieve it, especially when the stakes are high and the consequences really matter. It is about laying the groundwork for others' success, and then standing back and letting them shine."

Leadership is important because it inspires, motivates, and sets an example for people to accomplish positive changes in the world. They are able to inspire other individuals to reach their potential and obtain high levels of personal and professional success.

11

JOURNEY TO PROGRESS AND SUCCESS

"Failure is success in progress."

- Albert Einstein.

"Progress is not in enhancing what is, but in advancing toward what will be."

- Khalil Gibran.

"Success is not final; failure is not fatal: it is the courage to continue that counts." Winston Churchill.

Bill Gates was a software developer and an American Business Magnate who co-founded Microsoft with his friend Paul Allen. His success was a result of years of hard work. He wrote in his book, The Road Ahead, "Success is a lousy teacher. It seduces smart people into thinking they can't lose."

Bill Gates was passionate about programming since he was in class 8. His passion for computers persuaded him to learn more about software and hardware. He developed his skills through continuous practice. At the age of 17, he founded Traf-O-Data with his close friend and partner Paul Allen. Both of them shared a similar passion and interest in programming. Later in 1975, they founded their Startup Microsoft. Starting a new company was a big risk. Their passion, hard work, and meticulous planning helped them to move forward. In the initial stage, Microsoft didn't do well. They struggled to maintain their budget.

Their turning point was when Microsoft licensed MS-DOS an operating system to the personal computers of IBM, a giant in computers at that time. At this juncture, Bill Gates discontinued his studies at Harward to focus on his work at Microsoft. Subsequently, Microsoft became the biggest operating systems supplier across the globe. Microsoft kept developing its products and released Microsoft Office in 1990. It became the company's most successful office product and it became the most valued company in the world.

Generally, people assume progress as moving upward and getting better. Nevertheless, human progress is complex. What is perceived as progress in the short term may be devastating in the long run. It is not easy to define progress, however, we can understand progress easily through indicators of progress like higher education, a better status, improved health, raised income, better values, etc. Progress is a change towards a refined, improved, or desired state. For example, in sports progress refers to one's grasp of vital skills in a particular sport/game.

There is no standard definition of success. What means success to one can be different for another. For some success means obtaining a certain social status or fame, for some, it is pioneering something new, etc. Many people chase careers, money, or social status; however, they don't feel successful despite getting those things. Because one can measure success only when one is able to identify what drives one's happiness and whether it helps one to find purpose. Success comes with a balanced life.

How do you perceive Progress?

The desire for progress is a natural part of life. It is the onward movement toward a goal. People seek progress in different fields like change in careers, growth in investment & income, improving relationships, etc. Quite often these things do not happen as desired and hence lead to frustration. One must keep in mind progress is a process; it doesn't happen instantaneously. For example, losing weight, improving health, promotion, etc. takes time and requires consistent efforts.

According to George Bernard Shaw a playwright, critic, polemicist, and political activist, "Progress is impossible without change and those who cannot change their minds, cannot change anything." One must change to accomplish goals and achieve progress, in life. When you wish for something that you do not have, you have to change to obtain it. This is called the growth mindset.

Humans desire to progress, however, progress is not merely a mental game; it requires action to happen and a process to achieve it. One has to embrace consistent efforts to see positive change and progress. Progress is a requirement when a training programme is undertaken, or a project is designed. Our body adapts to the stress it puts under to achieve progress. In this process, if you are not constantly moving forward, you are likely to move backward. Hence achieving progress needs consistency.

You can make progress by working towards those goals that align with your life's mission. For example, you decide to do meditation every morning at 5.00 am. Currently, you have no fixed schedule and routine for meditation. First, you have to set a goal in your mind for doing meditation. Second, you have to work out a schedule to wake up every morning before 5.00 am to make it happen. Third, you should continue to do this exercise regularly as scheduled. Fourth, this exercise must lead to progressive change in your life.

According to H.L Mencken, "Change is not progress, but progress requires change. Thus, neither the Big Bang nor evolution necessarily implies progress, although I will argue that both have resulted in advancement. Mankind has made progress; improvements in society are indispensable and almost inevitable, and economic growth and progress are vital goals. The alternatives to progress are stagnation, deterioration, and the eventual extinction of all life." Progress is more than economic growth. It is a longer and better-quality life for a larger proportion of people.

Importance of Success:

Success is subjective. It cannot be measured in the matrix of success of some other person. What meant success to the industrialist and philanthropist Ratan Tata may not be success to the business tycoon Mukhesh Ambani. You can take some time to visualize and analyze what success really means to you. It may not conform to the traditional model. There is no requirement of proving to anyone about your success.

Success is intangible, it cannot be measured merely through material wealth. There are several instances where even beggars are multi-millionaires, but they spend their life in begging despite having more than enough wealth. There are several people who are billionaires and want to earn more and more at the cost of others without any value. They don't have any other goal other than accumulating more and more material wealth.

However, the mere accumulation of material wealth of such people can be called growth. They grow in life but do not experience satisfaction and happiness. Because success is not merely accumulating material wealth; it is collective growth, overall progress, and embracing humanity.

Success in the world is one thing and success in life is another.

You have to bring success to everything you do and not wait for it to arrive one day. There is no age limit, fixed time, or deadline for obtaining success in life. Some achieve success early in life, whereas many others achieve it in middle age or old age. Here are a few examples of successful people from different fields who were successful in life at different points in time in their life.

The world-famous Talk show personality Oprah Winnie was fired from her first broadcasting job at the age of 23. Internet entrepreneur, Jonah Peretti was a middle school teacher before founding his billion-dollar companies, Buzzfeed and The Huffington Post at the age of 30. American businessman, Colonel Sanders' fried chicken business KFC succeeded at the age of 62. Nelson Mandela became the President of South Africa at the age of 70 after spending 27 years in jail, etc.

The famous scientist and the father of modern physics, Albert Einstein once said, "Failure really is just success in progress. If you'd rather not to fail, you will probably never succeed." Michael Jordon the famous former International Basketball player said about his success, "I've missed more than 9000 shots in my career. I've lost almost 300 games. 26 times, I've been trusted to take the game-winning shot and missed. I've failed over and over and over again in my life. And that is why I succeeded."

Success comes from moments of disappointment, frustration, and failure. After you have gone through all those bitter times you become stronger and come closer to success. Abraham Lincoln suffered regularly from massive failures year after year. He failed in his business in the year 1831 and in the year 1836, he got a major nervous breakdown. Struggling for several years, he again failed in 1856 during US presidential elections. However, in 1861 he was elected as the sixteenth President of the USA.

Success delivers confidence, a sense of well-being, the ability to contribute at a greater level, hope, and leadership. For example, the continuation of a business or industry must be successful in creating new products, getting those products to the market, keeping clients, employees, and investors happy, and repeating that cycle, over and over. Because success is a journey and not a destination. Success is valuable, important, and necessary for survival.

Everyone wants to be successful, but only a few can achieve this because the route to success has many hurdles. Once you pass these hurdles, you are unstoppable. A successful person is a motivation for others. If you are successful, people will like you and follow you.

Success is the peak point on the ladder that people wish to climb. When you play the board game snake and ladder you are bitten by the snake many times especially when you reach easily towards the target. It is also true with success. The ladder of success is filled with trials, and one must face overcoming these hurdles.

You have to believe that you can successfully complete your work or a project and be successful in life. Belief in your capabilities will motivate you to move forward even if you fail. A group of boys happened to visit a village where they noticed a herd of elephants tied by a small rope tied to their forelegs. They were stunned by the fact that the huge elephants were not even giving try to break the rope and set themselves free.

The puzzled boys asked the mahout, why the elephants were not making any attempt to break the rope. He said, "When they were very small the same size rope was used to tie them and it was enough to hold them at that age. As they grew up, they were conditioned to believe that they could not break away. Now they believe that the rope can still hold them, so they never try to break free." In the same manner, many people do not work towards their success because they failed once and created a belief in their minds that achieving success is not their cup of tea.

Everyone has dreams and aspirations in their life. When these dreams come true, it is a success. If you have to make your dreams a reality, you need to work hard because success comes to those who deserve it. There is no shortcut to success. It requires consistent progress in hard work, dedication, teamwork, and values. Progress is the stepping stone to success.

Success in the world is one thing and success in life is another. You hardly find happiness, joy, and fun in successful people in the world. They are always sad because they missed procuring more wealth. Success in life is achieved when you have a smile that no one can take away, confidence that can never be shaken, and optimism that can never be influenced others.